For and against a united Ireland

FOR AND AGAINST A UNITED IRELAND

Fintan O'Toole
Sam McBride

Acadamh Ríoga na hÉireann
Royal Irish Academy

For and against a united Ireland

First published 2025
Royal Irish Academy, 19 Dawson Street, Dublin 2
ria.ie

© Royal Irish Academy
Text © Fintan O'Toole and Sam McBride, illustrations © Fergus Boylan

ISBN 9781802050356 (PB)
ISBN 9781802050363 (pdf)
ISBN 9781802050370 (epub)
ISBN 9781802050387 (audio)

All rights reserved. The material in this publication is protected by copyright law. Except as may be permitted by law, no part of the material may be reproduced (including by storage in a retrieval system) or transmitted in any form or by any means; adapted; rented or lent without the written permission of the copyright owners or a licence permitting restricted copying in Ireland issued by the Irish Copyright Licensing Agency CLG, 63 Patrick Street, Dún Laoghaire, Co. Dublin, A96 WF25.

Editors: Fiona Dunne and Brendan O'Brien
Cover design: Graham Thew
Index: Lisa Scholey

Printed in Poland by L&C Printing Group

General Product Safety Regulation (GPSR): For any safety queries, please contact us at productsafety@ria.ie

Royal Irish Academy is a member of Publishing Ireland, the Irish book publishers' association

To offset environmental impacts during the production of our books and journals we will plant 45 trees with Easy Treesie in 2025.

This is a project of:

5 4 3 2 1

For Philip Pettit.
Fintan O'Toole

For Kate and Patrick.
May you grow old in a land at peace in which you are respected and respect your neighbours, whatever its flag.
Sam McBride

Introduction ix

1. The case against a united Ireland — 1
FINTAN O'TOOLE

2. The case for a united Ireland — 33
SAM McBRIDE

3. The case for a united Ireland — 73
FINTAN O'TOOLE

4. The case against a united Ireland — 109
SAM McBRIDE

Postscript 149
Endnotes 155
Further reading 167
Acknowledgements 169
Index 171

Introduction

Usually, a book like this carries a disclaimer: the views expressed in it are strictly those of the authors. In this case, however, the opposite applies. In what follows, we have tried, in so far as is humanly possible, to keep our own views out of it. As journalists and newspaper columnists we know very well that complete objectivity is an impossible ideal. The subject of this book is often an emotive one and we each come to it with the conscious and unconscious biases we have inherited and inhabited. We grew up in different generations, one of us in Northern Ireland in a broadly unionist environment, the other in the Republic of Ireland in a broadly nationalist one. But we are emphatically *not* writing as representatives of those perspectives.

Necessarily, many of the arguments here do not express our personal views – they could not do so because they are purposefully self-contradictory. Rather, we are seeking to present what seem to us to be the most important arguments on each side. We made a very deliberate decision that, rather than one of us arguing for a united Ireland and the other against, we would each try to present, as fairly as we can, what we feel to be the best arguments for and against a united Ireland. We have tried not to put our fingers on the scales or to tilt the balance towards any outcome. In writing each case for and against, we have in mind the most contradictory of aims: that the reader will finish each of the chapters persuaded of the merits of their reasoning even though their logic has been directed towards opposing conclusions. Our hope is that seeing merit in arguments we do not instinctively like might be the basis for the kind of debate Ireland needs to have about its future: one founded on a respect for difference.

To say that these are what we perceive to be the best cases to be made for and against a united Ireland is not to say that they are the only ones. This is a short and, we hope, user-friendly overview of a complex set of issues surrounding the prospects of unification. It draws on very detailed work by many experts, especially those involved with the nonpartisan ARINS (Analysing and Researching Ireland North and South) project established in 2020 as a partnership between the Royal Irish Academy and the University of Notre Dame's Keough-Naughton Institute for Irish Studies. All of that work is available free of charge to the public and we recommend that those who want to go deeper into these questions should explore it.[1]

It is of course reasonable to ask: what is the point of embarking, as we have done here, on an intellectual journey that leads in opposite directions? We have to admit that for those who merely want to have their pre-existing opinions confirmed, there probably isn't one. Views about a united Ireland are, for many people, ciphers for other feelings about identity and belonging. The ghosts of history, religion, family and community hover around them. The traumas of the Troubles, and the still unreconciled bitterness they generated, continue to shape attitudes and give all of these questions a sharp emotional edge.

We respect those feelings and accept that they will always have a heavy bearing on the conduct of these debates. But we have one overarching shared feeling of our own, which is that emotion is

Introduction

not enough. Unification is not an inevitability, but it is a concrete possibility. Sooner or later, it is a question that everyone on the island – and everyone with any interest in Ireland – will likely have to engage with. And it is vital that this engagement is as rational as any political contest ever can be. The stakes – both positive and negative – are very high and we all need to have some idea as to what cards are on each side of the table.

Many people state with unbending assurance that a referendum on Irish unity will be held within a short number of years. Others hold with equal confidence that a border poll will not be held for some decades. (We use the terms 'referendum' and 'border poll' interchangeably – the first tends to be used more often in the South, the second in the North. It is important to note, however, that in reality there would be two votes, one on each side of the border.) Neither side is sure of what it claims to know. But the possibility of a referendum is ever-present. It is not just on the horizon – it affects the way people think about a wide range of political, social and cultural issues in the here and now.

Yet it is shot through with uncertainty. The secretary of state for Northern Ireland retains the power to call a referendum at any point and for any reason. Much debate focuses on the Good Friday Agreement's compulsion on that minister to consult voters if it seems to her or him that the public would vote for a united Ireland. But in an increasingly unpredictable world, we should be aware of the possibility that a mad or bad or impulsive secretary of state could decide at any moment to bring this debate to a head.

Anyone who cares for the future of this island ought to wish that such a campaign will be conducted so as to encourage honest debate and to enable both sides to believe they were able fairly and honestly to make the best case they could. Whatever happens, 'loser's consent' – the willingness of those disappointed by the outcome to live with it because they accept that it is the freely expressed desire of the majority – will be vital to the future peace and prosperity of everyone on the island.

There are ideologues on both sides who don't share this view. They want to win at all costs. In some cases, they have been – or remain – willing to kill their neighbours to advance their political goal. In a referendum campaign, they will shout loudest, and their voice will be heard. That is right, because this decision will involve all of society. But if only the most tribally partisan arguments were considered, that campaign would be a failure, regardless of who won.

This book is for everyone who has a stake in this momentous decision. But it is especially for the undecideds – the broad and growing body of citizens on both sides of the border who are open to the best rational arguments, rather than being already irreversibly committed to backing one side or the other regardless of whether that is to their material, social or cultural benefit.

In this book, each of us separately sets out what to him seem like the strongest arguments in favour of a united Ireland and the best arguments in favour of continuing with partition. We are not pushing you to change your mind, but we are urging you to open it. Unlike an election, the consequences of which will rest on our heads alone, this plebiscite will decide the future for generations yet unborn. It deserves to be treated with the respectful knowledge that our offspring and our neighbours will live or die, prosper or be impoverished, flourish or be repressed based not just on *what* is decided, but on *how* the decision is taken.

The tone of the debate will shape the decades after a border poll. A triumphal or sectarian approach is stupid not just from the perspective of the two sides involved. It would deposit a residue of instability and resentment that could result not in the desired settlement of historically vexed questions, but in a continuing sense of unsettlement that would leave profound problems for future generations to grapple with.

For any society to advance, it needs honestly to confront reality. Irrespective of how difficult that reality might be, the alternative is make-believe. Comforting as ignorance may be in the short term, it ultimately can't supplant facts.

As authors, we share a belief in rational enquiry, in honest debate, and above all in deciding this island's future by peaceful, democratic means.

Introduction

What we have written will have errors and omissions, as is inherent to all human endeavour. Both of us are white, male and born on the island – and therefore conditioned by experiences and assumptions that a majority of the population does not share. But please believe that whatever we have missed, misunderstood or misinterpreted is because of our own inadequacies, not because we are seeking to steer you towards one or other outcome.

In all likelihood, some of the questions we are seeking to answer will in time seem to be the wrong ones. In 1987, an academic surveying the future of Northern Ireland pronounced the discovery of coal as a crucial breakthrough because it was an indigenous source of energy. Now coal is irrelevant to energy security as we realise the harm its burning does to the environment.

Even as we write, the tectonic plates of geopolitics are shifting and long-established relationships between Europe, America and the rest of the world are being thrown into doubt and confusion. The vote on a united Ireland, whenever it comes, will take place in an international environment that is currently unknowable and in all probability very different from one envisaged in 1998, when the Belfast Agreement set the stage for a future border poll. Even with what we now know, it is likely that if a referendum is held in the middle of this century the dominant social and political issue will be coping with the effects of dramatic climatic shifts. In a context where parts of the world we now view as idyllic will probably be uninhabitable, triggering mass population movements, our successors might see this question in a context that makes much of the present debate seem like a quaint dispute.

Hundreds of years of historical hope and pain will weigh on a border poll campaign, and manifest themselves in the joy and the anguish, the thrill and the fear that will follow its result. We owe it to each other, and to all those who have suffered because of the tensions and passions aroused by these issues, to consider them thoughtfully and respectfully. Not everyone who went before us had this chance.

1.
The case against a united Ireland

FINTAN O'TOOLE

Is partition unnatural?

There is nothing natural about nations. They are products as much of history as of geography. But Ireland's physical shape as an island in the Atlantic seems to make its own case for political unity. Partition, in the nationalist imagination, is at heart a crime against nature. In 1982, Gerry Fitt, former leader of the Social Democratic and Labour Party (SDLP), told the House of Commons that 'Northern Ireland is an unnatural state'.[1] In 2017, Sinn Féin MEP Matt Carthy spoke of 'the undemocratic, unnatural and unjust nature of Partition'.[2]

Both were repeating a long-established claim. In March 1949, Ireland's then minister for external affairs, Seán MacBride, wrote to his British counterpart, Ernest Bevin, and quoted an unlikely source, the *Daily Mail*: 'The division of Ireland is unnatural. The split is a geographic and economic absurdity.' MacBride pointed to what he thought of as an undeniable truth: 'We have more clearly defined boundaries than most countries; the seas that surround our island provide those.'[3] He in turn was echoing Arthur Griffith, who wrote in 1904 that 'the frontier of Ireland has been fixed by nature'.[4]

The idea of the 'unnatural division of this country'[5] evokes the feeling that partition is not merely a political injustice but an offence against the God who established those clear and obvious boundaries. Father Michael O'Flanagan, vice-president of Sinn Féin, in a speech in Derry city in May 1921 insisted that 'The boundaries of Ireland were marked by the finger of Almighty God when He surrounded it with the circling sea.'[6]

Partition could also be imagined as a kind of vivisection. When it was being planned, *The Irish Times* asserted that 'You can no more dissect [Ireland] into two separate parts than you can divide the living body. Yet this is what ostensibly has been done. It is against reason, against history, against the very nature of things.'[7]

Yet, by this logic, Scottish and Welsh nationalism are entirely illegitimate: Britain, too, is 'surrounded with the circling sea' and intended by the Almighty to be a single polity. Irish nationalists have been reluctant to apply to their neighbouring island the geographical determinism they seek to impose on their own. Nor does the idea that an island is a natural political entity bear much scrutiny on a map of the world that includes New Guinea (divided between Papua and Indonesia), Borneo (Indonesia, Malaysia and Brunei), Hispaniola (Dominican Republic and Haiti) and Timor (divided between Indonesia and East Timor, whose long, heroic and ultimately successful struggle for independence would also be 'unnatural' by Irish nationalist criteria). Some large islands (Iceland, for example) are governed as single independent states; some (like the Japanese or Indonesian islands) are constituent parts of single country spread across an archipelago; some are split between different states. Being surrounded by sea is not a predictor of political fate.

Ireland, moreover, has never been unified as a functioning and independent political entity. Gaelic Ireland had high kings, from the tenth century to the Norman invasion of 1169, generally – and almost comically – listed in the contemporary annals as 'with opposition'. But no serious historian believes there was ever a single monarch whose rule was effective over the entire island. This contrasts sharply with, for example, Scotland, which operated as a separate kingdom for close to 800 years. The Lordship of Ireland and the Kingdom of Ireland, which did treat the island as a political entity, were creations of the English (later the British) monarchy.

Talk of the 'reunification' of Ireland rests on the technicality that an all-island Irish Free State did exist – for a single day. The Anglo-Irish Treaty of 1921 allowed the parliament of Northern Ireland to opt out of it, which it duly did on the day after the Irish Free State came into being on 6 December 1922. It was never going to do otherwise. An all-island Free State had no reality beyond the realms of wishful thinking.

Partition was, of course, messy, contradictory, incoherent and accompanied by violence. But there was nothing unusual in this. There were 24 independent states in Europe in 1900. There are now 45. Few of those new countries were lucky enough to emerge from orderly democratic processes. Most resulted from the implosion of empires (Ottoman, German, Austro-Hungarian, Russian and Soviet), from the most murderous conflicts the world has seen (the two World Wars) and from horrific civil wars or regional conflicts (the Greco-Turkish war; the break-up of Yugoslavia). Most left ethnic and/or religious minorities stranded on the 'wrong' side of borders. There are, for example, two million Hungarians in Romania and another million in Serbia, Ukraine and Slovakia. Catholics stranded in the North of Ireland and Protestants in the South may have had good reason to feel abandoned, but they were certainly not alone in twentieth-century Europe.

It is undoubtedly true that the creation of Northern Ireland in 1921 was a paradoxical outcome of Ireland's struggles for autonomy or independence: it created a devolved political entity for the very people who had resisted devolution most determinedly. As Northern Ireland's first prime minister, James Craig, acknowledged: 'The whole structure and ethos of Ulster unionism had been based upon a single object – determined opposition to Home Rule – and no constructive philosophy had been developed to govern a state they had neither expected nor wanted.'[8] But it is also true that, however much partition was officially unwanted, it suited ruling elites on both sides of the border.

It did so because it meant that neither of the two polities was under any great pressure to make itself into a genuinely pluralist democracy. Partition gave Northern Ireland a Protestant majority of 2:1. The Catholic minority was concentrated west of Lough Neagh and the River Bann, in south Armagh and south Down, in the Glens of Antrim, and in specific working-class areas of Belfast, creating a significant degree of geographical separation. In the Free State, Protestants formed less than 8% of the population in 1926 and their numbers were in steady decline. Independent Ireland was free to form its political and social identity around a fusion of nationalism with Catholicism.

However much partition might be decried in the rhetoric of Southern politicians, it was clear that the majority of the population prioritised the specifically Catholic character of the state over any gestures towards unification. In 1986 the then taoiseach Garret FitzGerald, who had long characterised the Irish Constitution's ban on divorce – its most flagrant encoding of a specifically Catholic doctrine – as an obstacle to reconciliation with Ulster Protestants, proposed a referendum to allow for the introduction of a very restrictive regime for the dissolution of marriage. His proposal was denounced by the Catholic hierarchy and by priests from the pulpit. Divorce was comprehensively rejected in the referendum, with two-thirds of voters rejecting the proposal. It was not until 1995 that the ban on divorce was removed from the Constitution, and even then it was by a tiny margin of fewer than 10,000 votes. In song, Southerners might occasionally mourn the loss of their fourth green field. In reality, they were happy enough with three.

Who are the people?

Underlying the desire for a united Ireland is the belief that there is such an entity as 'the Irish people'. A single people should have a single state. But things are not so simple. The idea of 'the people' in Irish law is complex and sometimes contradictory. Colin Harvey notes that 'It is striking how often "the people" is deployed as a concept within the language of the current framework' of discussions about the constitutional future.[9] But as Ivor Jennings put it, 'Let the people decide' is not a great shortcut to the resolution of conflicts 'because the people cannot decide until someone decides who are the people'.[10] Deciding who the people are is, in Ireland, much harder than it seems.

The preamble to the Irish Constitution, which serves as its fundamental enacting clause, echoes the more famous preamble to the American Constitution: 'We the People of the United States ...'. But it does so in ways that are rather more problematic. First, this evocation of popular sovereignty does not come first. It is preceded by a bald statement that the authority of the people is subordinate to that of 'the Most Holy Trinity, from Whom is all authority and to Whom, as our final end, all actions both of men and States must be referred'. A theological doctrine provides the ultimate frame of reference.

Second, the people who are giving themselves the Constitution are 'We, the people of Éire …'. As Oran Doyle puts it, 'the people entitled to vote in the [1937] plebiscite and to whom the Constitution would first apply were located on only part of the island of Ireland, representing a significant retrenchment on claims of an all-island Irish identity'.[11]

Third, and most importantly, 'the people' are implicitly understood as Catholic and nationalist. The preamble goes on to acknowledge 'all our obligations to our Divine Lord, Jesus Christ, Who sustained our fathers through centuries of trial' – an obvious reference to the disabilities suffered by Catholics under the Penal Laws. And it conjures a people 'Gratefully remembering their heroic and unremitting struggle to regain the rightful independence of our Nation'. Those who did not wish to see an independent Ireland are not included in 'our' nation.

This preamble was largely inspired by a draft created by the Jesuit Order's Irish province. Mr Justice Gerard Hogan, in his definitive *The Origins of the Irish Constitution 1928–1941*, writes that 'The Jesuit document proved to be enormously influential … The first four lines of the Preamble closely follow the Jesuit … model.'[12] It is thus hardly surprising that the Constitution reflects a conception of 'the people' that emphasises its particular character as a religious community.

The changes to Articles 2 and 3 of the Constitution that followed the signing of the Belfast Agreement of 1998 undoubtedly alter and broaden this idea of who the Irish people are. The new articles emphasise the 'birthright of every person born in the island of Ireland, which includes its islands and seas, to be part of the Irish Nation'. They declare the desire of the Irish nation 'to unite all the people who share the territory of the island of Ireland, in all the diversity of their identities and traditions'. And they assert the nation's 'special affinity with people of Irish ancestry living abroad who share its cultural identity and heritage'.

The Constitution therefore seems to gesture towards three distinct ideas of who 'the Irish people' are. One, still there in its unreconstructed form in the preamble, implicitly defines them as

The case against a united Ireland

the Catholic and nationalist inhabitants of the 26 counties. The second envisages them as the whole population of the island, no longer defined as Catholic and nationalist but rather as belonging to an unspecified number of different traditions. And the third nods towards the idea that the Irish people might not even be a concept confined to the island itself but might also encompass the descendants of Irish immigrants in other countries.

There's nothing innately wrong with such a multilayered notion of 'the people', and the ambiguities are arguably true to the slippery complexities of Irish history. But in the context of thinking about a united Ireland, the necessity for these shifting definitions suggests that the argument that there must be one state because there is one people stands on decidedly unstable ground. And that's before we get to that even trickier concept: the 'people of Northern Ireland'.

This, too, has deep political and legal foundations. For Northern Ireland's prime minister Basil Brooke, the legitimacy of partition rested upon 'the declared will of the Northern Ireland people, expressed through their elected Parliament'.[13] In 1973, the Sunningdale Agreement contained parallel declarations by the British and Irish governments that used the term 'the people of Northern Ireland' three times in one key clause alone: 'The Irish Government fully accepted and solemnly declared that there could be no change in the status of Northern Ireland until a majority of the people of Northern Ireland desired a change in that status. The British Government solemnly declared that it was, and would remain, their policy to support the wishes of the majority of the people of Northern Ireland. The present status of Northern Ireland is that it is part of the United Kingdom. If in the future the majority of the people of Northern Ireland should indicate a wish to become part of a united Ireland, the British Government would support that wish.'

It is notable that, in the same declaration, the Irish government explicitly put itself forward as speaking for 'The people of the Republic, together with a minority in Northern Ireland' – another very complicated idea in which the inhabitants of the Republic formed a 'people' that could be joined to the Catholic/nationalist minority north of the border but that was a separate concept to 'the people of Northern Ireland'.

If anything, the Belfast Agreement made things even more uncertain. It refers in its opening declaration to 'the people, North and South', as though there is indeed a single entity with two parts. But it goes on to rest the big decisions on the future of the island on 'the legitimacy of whatever choice is freely exercised by a majority of the people of Northern Ireland'. And then in one single clause it seems to evoke three different concepts of the people: 'while a substantial section of the people in Northern Ireland share the legitimate wish of a majority of the people of the island of Ireland for a united Ireland, the present wish of a majority of the people of Northern Ireland, freely exercised and legitimate, is to maintain the Union'.[14] So there are the people *in* Northern Ireland, the people *of* Northern Ireland, and the people of the *island* of Ireland.

This may all be somewhat mind-boggling, but it is not merely theoretical. In June 2016, the 'people of Northern Ireland' voted by 56% to 44% to remain in the European Union. This surely was an expression of political identity 'freely exercised and legitimate'. Yet it was deemed to have no real standing. The UK's Supreme Court ruled in a 2017 decision that the Belfast Agreement's principle of consent did not extend beyond the question of Northern Ireland's status as part of the United Kingdom.[15] As the majority ruling put it, 'section 1 [of the Northern Ireland Act of 1998], which gave the people of Northern Ireland the right to determine whether to remain part of the UK or to become part of a united Ireland, does not regulate any other change in the constitutional status of Northern Ireland'. Thus, the 'people of Northern Ireland' seem to be a sovereign people – but only in relation to the possibility of a united Ireland. In every other respect, they are not free to exercise their own choices about where they belong. They are a 'people' whose political existence is visible only in one very special kind of light.

All of this means that the whole idea of who makes up the people of Ireland, of the island and of Northern Ireland is shifty

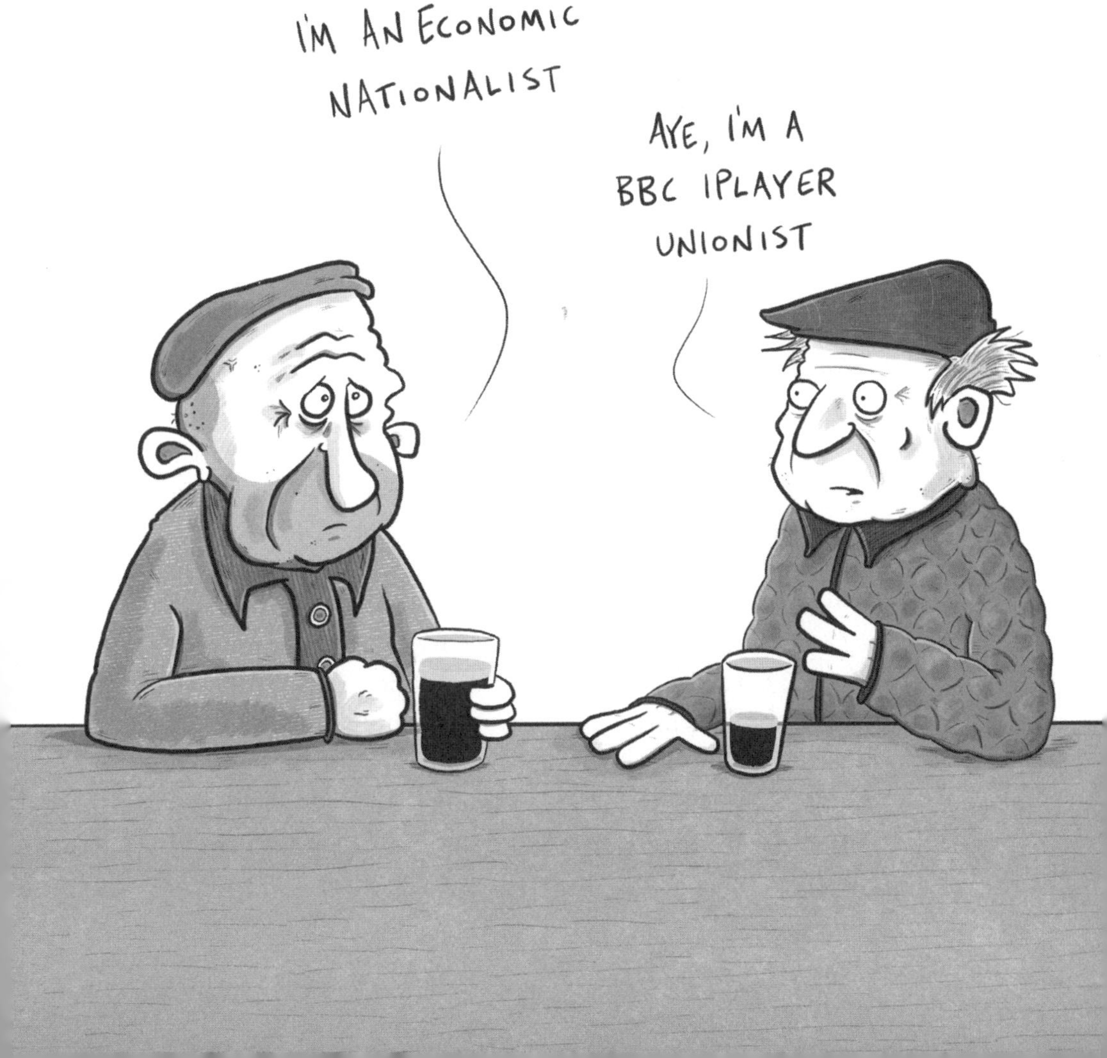
I'M AN ECONOMIC NATIONALIST
AYE, I'M A BBC IPLAYER UNIONIST

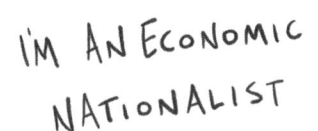

and blurred. The principle of popular sovereignty ought to give us a solid foundation for the innate rightness of a united Ireland. On the contrary, however, it merely reminds us that historical and political necessities and desires constitute 'the people' – and not the other way around.

Thus those who wish to see a united Ireland can rely neither on the idea that it is a natural condition nor on any simple belief that there is a single people that must automatically exist within a single state. They have to base their arguments on practicalities. Is a united Ireland politically feasible? And how would it improve the lives of those who would live in it? One participant in the ARINS focus group study in 2022 said of a united Ireland that they wanted to know 'exactly what it would look like. Not like Brexit, but exactly how it would look before it was passed', while another flatly suggested that 'I would prefer no change to unknown change.'[16] There are good reasons to think that 'unknown change' is what is currently on offer.

Will there be violence?

The most difficult issue to discuss in relation to the prospect of a united Ireland is violence. No one wants to suggest that armed groups – in this case loyalist paramilitaries – should be able to veto the democratic decisions taken by citizens. And yet the possibility of violent resistance weighs heavily on the minds of prospective Southern voters. Asked in the ARINS/*The Irish Times* survey of 2022 what they would need to know before voting in a border poll, those in the Republic identified as their single biggest concern 'whether a united Ireland would be peaceful'. This anxiety was identified by 66% of respondents, making it even more prominent in their minds than the economic effects of unification (57%).

Moreover, the Southern public 'is much more likely than its Northern counterpart to shy away from voting for unity when the prospect of Loyalist violence is raised: 42% are less likely and 18% more likely to vote for unity'.[17] It is striking that this fear of a violent backlash is so much more pronounced in the South than in the North – perhaps because of a belief that much of it might be directed at the Dublin government, its public servants and its institutions.

The Independent Reporting Commission that monitors paramilitary violence in Northern Ireland notes in its 2023 report that 'paramilitarism is different to what it was 25 years ago, but … it has continuing links to that previous reality also'. While much of it has descended into mere gangsterism, 'there is a residual political dimension to the continuation of paramilitarism today'. The commission reports that 'In respect of the ideological dimension of continuing paramilitarism, they have support in sections of the community as the "carriers of the torch" today and the defenders of a worldview shared by some in that community.'[18] Within loyalist paramilitarism the torch that is being carried is the adamant refusal to submit to being absorbed into a united Ireland.

Paramilitary-related violence has declined considerably but it has not gone away. There were 1,238 sectarian incidents recorded by the police in Northern Ireland in 2022–3. There have been between one and three paramilitary-related deaths per year in each of the past ten years, apart from 2016–17, when there were five. In the decade from 2013 to 2023, loyalists were responsible for 74 bombing incidents and 106 shootings. In 2022–3, 23 of the 32 paramilitary-style assaults (72%) were attributed to loyalists.

The evidence suggests that most people from a Protestant/unionist background would accept a majority vote in favour of a united Ireland. In the ARINS/*The Irish Times* survey of 2023, 52% said they would not be happy with such a result 'but could live with it'. However, 23% said they would find it 'almost impossible to accept'.[19] It would be wrong to assume that most of those people would resort to violent resistance, but we know only too well from Irish history that relatively small numbers of people, if sufficiently well organised and motivated, can create mayhem and cause immense harm. We also know that this violence can have an outsized influence on the political climate and that it can take on a dynamic of its own that is very hard to stop.

Northern Ireland has, in the loyalist paramilitaries, the core of an organisational structure for violent resistance to a united Ireland. It also has extremely high levels of gun ownership. In 2020, there were 55,441 firearm certificate holders in Northern Ireland.[20] In 2012, *The Detail* reported that these licensed gun owners (then amounting to almost 60,000) held over 146,000 weapons (not including those held by serving police and prison officers).[21] There are also, of course, an unknown number of illegally held guns.

Two obvious problems have to be confronted. The first is that, in the run-up to an ill-prepared border poll, there could be not just rioting and intercommunal violence in Northern Ireland but loyalist attacks south of the border. Given the level of anxiety already present among potential Southern voters, this could have serious consequences for both the conduct and the outcome of a referendum.

The other difficulty relates to what would happen after unification. Who could police areas of Northern Ireland where loyalist paramilitaries have their strongholds? The pronounced preference of Southern voters is for one set of institutions and services to operate in a united Ireland – so presumably the Garda Síochána would have to do so with, in an extreme scenario, the support of the Irish army. The Garda, unlike the Police Service of Northern Ireland (PSNI), is essentially an unarmed force. It seems highly unlikely that most people in the South are mentally prepared for the prospect of its members facing off against armed loyalist paramilitaries.

The possibility of violence is enhanced by the nature of the border poll as envisaged in the Belfast Agreement. It would be a simple majority vote, making it possible that unification could be agreed by a tiny margin – in principle one vote could swing it. It is easy to see how such a narrow victory could be construed as illegitimate with claims (valid or otherwise) of outside interference or voter fraud amplified by social media disinformation and AI (artificial intelligence)-generated images.

The threat of serious violence could be diminished if the shape of a unified Ireland were made clear in advance of a poll and, critically, if that shape were one in which those who wish to retain a

British allegiance were reassured by generous concessions to their sense of identity. But there is no great reason to believe that people in the Republic are in general prepared to make those concessions.

What political institutions would govern a united Ireland?

A deliberative forum was organised in 2021, designed to tease out the views of a representative sample of Southerners about how Irish unity might happen and what it might look like. Strikingly, of the 46 people who participated, 28 'indicated before the deliberations that they were either not at all or not very well informed' about the issues. 'Generally, the participants were surprised to learn that there are different possible versions of a united Ireland.'[22] This in itself is telling. There are reasons to believe that for most people in the South a united Ireland is, as Hamlet would put it, 'a consummation/Devoutly to be wished' rather than a practical proposition they have considered in any depth.

There is no doubt that the devout wish for a united Ireland is a core part of the majority identity on the island, and especially in the Republic. The desire for it is sincere and entirely legitimate. But a good way to think about it might be to compare it with attitudes towards the Irish language. This, too, is a core part of the majority identity. In a typical survey (in this case one taken for Údarás na Gaeltachta in November 2024), almost three-quarters (73%) of respondents said they 'believe Irish is essential to Irish identity'.[23] But two-thirds expressed regret over not having better spoken Irish – suggesting that they have not done very much to make this 'essential' aspect of their cultural identity a real part of their lives.

This is borne out by figures from the 2022 Census, which show that just 10% of the population speaks Irish very well and that the number of daily speakers of Irish outside the education system numbered a mere 71,968. In other words, it is perfectly possible to have a strong attachment to an ideal of what it means to be Irish while having at best only a passive commitment to what the achievement of that ideal might entail. This is as true of a united Ireland as it is of the Irish language.

An arresting finding of the ARINS/*The Irish Times* surveys is that only 29% of citizens in the Republic had taken a day trip to the North either several times or lots of times in the five years before 2022, in contrast with the comparable figure of 65% of Northerners who have spent the equivalent amount of time in the South. Half of Southerners had taken no day trips across the border at all and two-thirds said they had no friends in the North.[24] Southerners may want to unite with the North but they don't speak Northern.

This is the context in which participants in the deliberative forum from the Republic might well be surprised to learn that there are different versions of a united Ireland. There are, in particular, two distinctive models: integration and devolution. In the first, Northern Ireland would cease to exist in any form and would simply be absorbed into the existing 26-county state. There would be one parliament (in Dublin) and (presumably after a period of transition) all laws, courts, public institutions and public services would operate in the same way across the whole island.

In the second model, Northern Ireland would continue to exist as a devolved entity, somewhat like Wales within Britain now. The central government in Dublin would be sovereign and would deal with national taxation, social welfare, health policy, European Union (EU) matters, foreign and defence policy, climate change and large-scale infrastructural developments. The Irish Supreme Court (presumably now including judges from the North) would have overall authority to interpret the law and the Constitution. But what is now Northern Ireland would still have a power-sharing local administration in Belfast with its own limited yet nonetheless significant tax-raising powers, lower-level courts, perhaps a retained Police Service of Northern Ireland and perhaps its own flag, anthem and emblems.

An overwhelming majority of participants in the forum said they 'favoured telling voters before the referendum the specific model of

The case against a united Ireland

a united Ireland that was on offer'. As one participant put it, 'I don't think people will vote if they don't understand what they're voting for. They'll vote against it because they won't understand it.' This is indeed borne out by the experience of Irish referendums on complex questions: if people don't know exactly what the proposition means, they tend either to vote No or to stay at home.

Thus, if a border poll were not to be another Brexit-style exercise, it would have to offer voters a concrete sense of what kind of polity they were being asked to accept or reject. But this in itself complicates everything. Before negotiations on which model of unity is supposed to operate, the Dublin government would have to decide on, and create in the Republic a sufficient consensus behind, the specific model it is proposing.

Here, though, there are two very big problems. First, the Northern public is more supportive of the devolved model, while the Southern public favours integration. In particular, Protestants in Northern Ireland are 'extremely opposed to the integrated model' while 'Citizens in the Republic are much more in favour of the integrated model.'[25] Hence, one or other model would end up being imposed on parts of the population that don't want it. This does not look like a promising start to an inclusive and peaceful future for the island.

Second, within the Republic, there is a profound tension between what the Constitution seems to imply and what the Southern public seems to want. Most people in the South see a united Ireland as merely an extension of the state they currently inhabit. This reflects the demand for what Article 3 of the 1937 Constitution called 'the reintegration of the national territory'. But Article 3 was changed in a referendum in 1998 that was passed by 94% of voters. This idea of 'integration' was deleted and replaced with a declaration of 'the firm will of the Irish nation, in harmony and friendship, to unite all the people who share the territory of the island of Ireland, in all the diversity of their identities and traditions'.

This radically altered formulation suggests, first, that the island is to be shared rather than integrated and, second, that the political structures of a united Ireland should be ones that are purpose-built to accommodate a diversity of identities. A one-size-fits-all Dublin-centred government does not seem like a reasonable expression of this aspiration. It seems as though citizens in the Republic are (consciously or otherwise) hankering for the old Article 3 that they so comprehensively chose to scrap.

What about flags and anthems?

One participant in the deliberative forum in the Republic expressed a view that seems to be widely held by her compatriots on what might happen in the creation of a united Ireland: 'The symbols and national anthem and everything would be subject to negotiation. Why? If they think we're going to change our anthem and flag they've got another thing coming, so I don't know how they could even think about that.'[26] This use of 'they' is interesting – as opposed to 'our' national symbols, it implies both a profound sense of difference and an instinctive reluctance on the part of 'us' to make concessions to 'them'.

Flags and anthems might seem to be of little real significance. John Hume, in many ways the intellectual architect of the Belfast Agreement, liked to quote his father's dictum that 'You can't eat a flag': 'what he was saying is real politics is about the living standards, about social and economic development. It's not about waving flags at one another.'[27]

Many of us might wish that this were so. But flags, anthems and emblems have a remarkably strong effect on Southern attitudes to unity: in the ARINS/*The Irish Times* surveys, almost half of the public in the South (47% and 48%, respectively) say they would be less likely to vote for a united Ireland if it required the creation of a new national flag and national anthem.[28] It is notable, too, that 54% of Southerners would be less likely to vote for a united Ireland if it meant Ireland rejoining the Commonwealth, a move that would allow those of British identity in the new Ireland to retain a sense of connection to a history and a set of symbols that remain important to them.

Remarkably, this hostility extends to Northern motifs that one might expect to be seen as more inclusive. It is startling, for example, that even when Southern respondents in the ARINS/*The Irish Times* survey were specifically reminded that the Red Hand of Ulster is used by both the Northern Ireland soccer team and the Gaelic Athletic Association (which displays it on its own flag), they still express strongly negative feelings about it (52% give it a negative score, compared with just 17% who rank it positively).[29] One has to wonder whether this points not just to instinctive hostility towards symbols of Britishness, but to an underlying antipathy towards any symbols of Northern-ness.

What this apparent antagonism suggests is that most people in the Republic want a united Ireland – but only if it does not involve them making any real compromises on their own symbolic attachments. This, too, is at odds with the meaning of the Belfast Agreement. A cornerstone of that agreement is the commitment to 'recognise the birthright of all the people of Northern Ireland to identify themselves *and be accepted as* Irish or British, or both, as they may so choose, and accordingly confirm that their right to hold both British and Irish citizenship is accepted by both Governments and would not be affected by any future change in the status of Northern Ireland'.[30]

This means that the advent of a united Ireland would not in any way diminish the rights of those in the North who wish not only to continue to hold a British identity but – crucially – to have that Britishness 'accepted' by the Irish government. What does 'acceptance' mean in this context? It implies a positive desire to give formal recognition to the way those from a Protestant/unionist background choose to 'identify themselves', which would surely include the British crown, flag and anthem and perhaps also emblems of Ulster like the Red Hand.

But it also implies a careful self-restraint in not demanding that people give their allegiance to symbols they have long regarded as hostile. Whatever the noble intentions of the tricolour, with its colour-coded expression of amity between the Green and Orange, it has also long functioned in Northern Ireland as a tribal marker.

And it does not seem to be in the spirit of the Belfast Agreement to expect those who have a British identity to sing an anthem in Irish about their willingness to kill and die for *Seantír ár sinsear*, the ancient land of their ancestors – a phrase in the anthem that, for them, might evoke Scotland or England.

The Belfast Agreement requires any future Irish government that becomes the sovereign power in what is now Northern Ireland to show 'rigorous impartiality' in relation to the 'identity, ethos and aspirations of both communities'. This obligation seems flatly incompatible with the retention in a united Ireland of the current symbols of Irish national identity. But every poll on this issue in the South – not just the ARINS surveys but polls for *The Sunday Business Post* and for *The Irish Times* (both in 2022) – have shown that those symbols really matter to voters in the Republic. There is an irreconcilable contradiction between the way Southerners see a united Ireland – essentially as a Greater 26 Counties – and the way it would have to function on the levels both of institutions and of symbols.

What are the financial implications for the Republic?

All of this is not to say that Hume's contention that 'real politics is about the living standard' is irrelevant. Money matters. Feelings about identity, belonging, history and culture shape attitudes to Irish unity – but so do more concrete perceptions of financial costs and benefits. In the ARINS/*The Irish Times* survey in 2022, almost half (48%) of respondents in the Republic say they would be less likely to vote for unification if a united Ireland led to them being €4,000 a year worse off. In the 2023 survey, the figure was 44%. This is hardly surprising: the Republic has become a relatively prosperous society, but it is not so rich that most families would not find such a loss very difficult to manage. The median annual income of all workers in the South in 2023 was €43,221, so this would represent a loss of close to a tenth of typical before-tax earnings.

The case against a united Ireland

The potential cost of unity to the Republic is determined by the reality that Northern Ireland's devolved government spends more money than it raises internally and that the difference is made up by transfers from the UK government. In 2021, Northern Ireland had revenues of £19.3 billion and expenditures of £33.2 billion. It remained solvent because it received a subvention of £13.9 billion from London.[31] This transfer represents more than a quarter (28%) of Northern Ireland's Gross Domestic Product (GDP).

It is true that some of what is counted as expenditure by Northern Ireland (contributions to the UK's defence budget, for example, or to interest payments on the UK's national debt) would not apply in a united Ireland – but on the other hand, public sector wages and welfare payments would have to rise to the higher levels that are current south of the border. Economists John FitzGerald and Edgar Morgenroth have estimated that these latter costs would amount (on the basis of the rates that applied in 2021) to pay rises of £4.2 billion and welfare increases of £3.8 billion.

In May 2024, FitzGerald and Morgenroth told the Oireachtas Committee on the Implementation of the Good Friday Agreement that the overall effect of these subtractions and additions is that 'the transfer to the North would be around £1.1billion (€1.2 bn) lower in a united Ireland, amounting to around £9.6 billion (€10.9 bn) or around 5% of Irish national income'.[32] But if the costs of increased public sector wages and welfare rates are included, they calculate that 'the cost to Ireland of supporting Northern Ireland within a united Ireland [rises] to almost 10% of [national income]. This is a huge sum as total government expenditure in Ireland currently amounts to around 40% of [national income]. This would add a quarter to public expenditure in Ireland, while producing a very limited increase in revenue. To deal with the resulting deficit, which under the most favourable circumstances would persist for many years after unification, there would have to be a dramatic increase in taxation and/or a major reduction in expenditure.'[33]

Would voters in the South be happy to accept higher taxes as the price for unity? There is little evidence from surveys that they would. A poll for the *Irish Independent* in May 2021 found that

'In the Republic, 54% said they would be unwilling to pay more tax to fund a United Ireland. Just 22% said they would pay more while 24% didn't know.'[34] A Red C poll for the *Business Post* in November the same year found that 'just 41% would support a united Ireland if it meant increased taxes, meaning when undecided voters are removed that less than half of all adults expressing an opinion (48%) support this'. It is notable that in the same poll, a little over half of Sinn Féin supporters expressed a willingness to pay higher taxes for a united Ireland.[35]

The only way to limit the costs to the Republic, and its consequent need for higher taxes, lower public spending or both, is for the UK to continue to pay for at least two parts of the North's expenditure after Irish unification: Northern Ireland's share of the UK's national debt and pensions. Would this happen?

The norm when states break up is that the national debt is divided proportionally. This was the case when the Irish Free State was established in 1922. (The liability was cancelled in 1925 largely to compensate the Free State for its failure to secure significant adjustments to the border through the Boundary Commission.) The Scottish government agreed in 2014 that if it succeeded in the referendum of that year, 'An independent Scottish state would become responsible for a fair and proportionate share of the UK's current liabilities.'[36] That share was estimated at the time at £130 billion (€157 billion). Apart altogether from the direct financial consequences of effectively cancelling this debt for Northern Ireland, the UK would surely be reluctant to set a radically different precedent for a united Ireland, which would incentivise future moves towards independence by Wales and Scotland by suggesting that they could leave their shares of UK debt behind.

As for pension payments, the UK funds them on an annual basis from social insurance contributions. As FitzGerald and Morgenroth put it, 'The social insurance pensions paid out in the UK are generally equal to the insurance contributions paid in each year. The idea that the UK would continue to pay pensions while a united Ireland collected the related social insurance contributions seems most improbable.'[37]

As with the idea that the UK would relieve a united Ireland of the cost of servicing Northern Ireland's share of the debt, it is improbable because it depends on the willingness of the voters of southern England to commit themselves over the long term to transferring large amounts of their taxes to what would now be a foreign country. The experience of Brexit, in which both resentment of payments to the EU and indifference to the specific conditions of Northern Ireland were starkly obvious, does not point to the existence of any such enthusiasm. Some spirit of generosity could well be generated around the moment of separation but expecting it to continue over the long term seems remarkably naive.

The very best that might be hoped for is some kind of deal in which there is a trade-off of liabilities, with the UK, for example, agreeing to keep paying pensions for a decade after unification provided Ireland takes over Northern Ireland's share of the debt. Yet even if negotiations were successful in reducing the costs of unification to the Irish exchequer, they would probably take no more than a few billion off the €20 billion it would have to find each year until some point in the future when Northern Ireland's economy is as productive as the Republic's. A combination of substantially higher taxes, reduced government spending (including on badly needed long-term investment in housing, transport and energy and water infrastructure) and higher levels of public borrowing would be required. These measures would create precisely the reduction in living standards that most voters in the South regard as a price not worth paying for Irish unity.

What about social welfare?

For a long time, the Republic's social welfare system was essentially a watered-down and less generous version of the UK's. But the two systems now differ in two substantial ways. In the event of a united Ireland, these differences would have serious implications for those who depend on benefits – and those who fund those benefits through their taxes.

First, in the North, many more benefits are means-tested, and many more families depend on them: half of households in Northern Ireland are eligible for a means-tested benefit compared with just a quarter in the Republic. And second, the level of the payments that are not means-tested is much higher in the South. The standard rate of unemployment benefit in the Republic is more than twice the rate in the North while the non-contributory state pension is about 2.5 times as large.[38] As Ciara Fitzpatrick and Charles O'Sullivan put it, 'this leaves many unanswerable questions, the first of which is whether a shared future will be one of increased co-operation or a completely unified social security system'.[39]

Increased cooperation might well be possible for a limited period after unification, but it seems implausible that a single state could continue to run two very different welfare systems for very long. They would have to be combined into a single set of benefits and entitlements. But this would be formidably difficult. Does a unified Irish state bring everyone in the North up to its much higher payments? This would be very expensive but perhaps manageable. But does it then eliminate or reduce the means-tested benefits that people in Northern Ireland currently receive? This could leave many vulnerable families in serious distress.

There's an even more fundamental problem. Most people in the North are used to being net beneficiaries of the tax and welfare systems. Four-fifths of households in Northern Ireland receive more in benefits than they pay in taxes, compared with slightly more than half in the Republic. It does not seem plausible that people in the Republic would be willing to accept that the bulk of the Northern population could continue to receive more than it contributes while a much smaller proportion of the Southern population does so.

What would the health service look like?

Politicians and political scientists are naturally inclined to imagine that the most important issue in thinking about a united Ireland

The case against a united Ireland

is the nature of its political institutions. But for potential voters in parallel border polls – and especially for those in Northern Ireland – by far the most important question is the fate of the National Health Service. Some 50% of Northerners say they are more likely to vote for unity if a united Ireland adopted the type of health system used in the UK, and only 3% would be less likely to do so. This 'NHS effect' has a larger bearing on how people think they might vote even than telling them that they would be £3,500 (€4,000) better off in a united Ireland.[40]

The consequences of unity for the delivery of healthcare are also a major concern south of the border: 60% of Northerners and 57% of Southerners listed healthcare among the top two issues they would need to know more about before voting in a referendum. Similarly, in focus groups, the issue that 'arose spontaneously' (without prompting from moderators) was 'most frequently the health system'.

What was clear from those discussions is that nothing is really very clear. On the one hand, people on both sides have an acute awareness that the two jurisdictions have very different health systems. On the other, they were quite unsure about how those systems work in practice – let alone how they might be integrated.

Typical comments on health from the Northern Ireland groups were that 'You'd have to pay for your doctor [in a united Ireland], or you'd have to pay for your dentist'; and 'Well obviously we get it free and down there doesn't. What is it, £50 to go to see a doctor, then so much for a prescription afterwards.' In the Southern groups there were comments such as 'As it is, our health service is no matter where you go hospital, doctor, dentist, you have to pay for it, in Northern Ireland you don't'; that in Northern Ireland 'you don't have to pay to go to see your GP, you don't have to pay to go to the hospital, that is one good aspect of the overall picture of Northern Ireland'; and that 'They have a great thing going with the NHS.'[41]

As Jennifer Todd, Joanne McEvoy and John Doyle put it in their analysis of the focus group results, 'For many participants there was no nuance on the question of health—it was a mythical NHS in the North and it was assumed that everyone, regardless of income or health condition, paid for every health service in the South.' In fact, much of the Southern health service is free at the point of delivery for large parts of the population, while the NHS has in recent years struggled to deliver in practice the free care it promises in principle. (As of September 2023, 545,000 people were waiting for elective care in Northern Ireland.)[42] Male life expectancy at birth is now 81.3 years in the Republic, while female life expectancy at birth is 84.5 years. In the North, the equivalent figures are 78.8 years and 82.5 years.[43]

And much of what people on either side of the border have in common is a shared frustration that neither health service is up to scratch: 'Significantly, a number of participants changed their position in the middle of a single contribution, starting off with a robust defence of the NHS, assuming everything was private in the South and ending up saying that there was little difference in reality, due to non-availability.'

What is obvious, nonetheless, is that Northerners would be very unlikely to vote for a united Ireland if it meant that they would lose the NHS and have to take their chances with the way healthcare operates south of the border. As Brendan O'Leary and John Garry put it in their analysis of the ARINS research: 'Adopting the Southern health system would be a massive turn-off for Northerners, and to a similar extent for Catholics and Protestants.'[44]

The apparently simple solution for advocates of a united Ireland is the creation of an all-Ireland NHS – what the campaign group Ireland's Future calls 'a world-class all island national health service'.[45] Sinn Féin proposes the creation of 'an all-Ireland Integration Committee to make preparations for the establishment of a National Health Service body, subsuming the functions currently carried out by the HSE in the South and the NHS in the North'.[46]

However desirable the aim of a single NHS for the whole island may be, two huge problems arise. One is that there has been little effort to figure out how the integration of existing services would work in practice. Health is already an established area of North–South cooperation under the Belfast Agreement of 1998. Almost

YEP, THAT'S RIGHT, IT DEFINITELY HAPPENED THIS SIDE OF THE BORDER
WELCOME TO NORTHERN IRELAND

all experts agree that, even in the absence of a united Ireland, it makes sense to share many high-level facilities. Yet, with rare exceptions like the Congenital Heart Disease Network and the North West Cancer Centre at Altnagelvin, little has been done. As Deirdre Heenan points out in her review of the existing health landscape for ARINS, 'the regular and repeated calls for further collaboration and co-operation have not been accompanied by any detailed plans, feasibility studies or robust data to support an all-island approach. Statements by political parties and policymakers urging improved cross-border working are expressed in general, vague terms.'[47] Given that the evidence strongly suggests that voters would expect a detailed healthcare plan *before* any border poll, this absence does not augur well.

The second big problem lies in the nature of the Southern health service itself. As Anne Matthews puts it, 'the health system in the Republic has major structural problems that constitute a significant barrier to practical cooperation' across the border – never mind full integration in a united Ireland.[48] It is a strange and unwieldy hybrid of public and private provision. In principle, everyone is entitled to free treatment as an inpatient or outpatient in a public hospital. Yet, as of January 2024, 2.4 million people – 45% of the entire population – had private health insurance.[49] There are ten private hospital groups operating in the Republic, some of them (like the Mater Private Group and St Vincent's University Hospital) intertwined with public hospitals, others standing alone. As a further complication, nearly a third of public hospitals are 'voluntary', some of them secular and others owned by Catholic religious orders.

As a consequence, the Republic has a two-tier healthcare system in which one half of the population can buy reasonably quick access to treatment while the other half has to endure long waiting lists. This hybrid system is extremely inefficient and opaque. No one fully understands how resources are being used. In October 2022, Leo Kearns, chair of the Regional Health Areas Advisory Group appointed by government to reconfigure the management of the public system, told the Joint Oireachtas Committee on Health that 'The way we have organised our health service is like we are playing a game of football and, first, we have not even marked out the pitch. Then, every single player on the pitch is reporting to somebody different. They are not reporting to the manager. They do not even know who that is.'[50]

Governments have tried at various times to bring some order to this chaos by abolishing regional health boards, creating a centralised Health Service Executive and proposing to transform the whole system into one based on a universal insurance model. None of these initiatives has worked: Dublin is now trying to devolve management back to regional structures and the universal insurance project was simply abandoned.

This raises an obvious question: if the Republic has been unable over many decades to integrate its own health service, how can we imagine it would be capable of amalgamating it with a service north of the border founded on very different ideological and organisational principles? Before creating an all-island NHS, the South would have to nationalise those ten private hospital groups. It would also have to end – or at least severely curtail – the private insurance system that supports them. It is not at all obvious either that it has the capacity to do this or that there would be sufficient political support among Southern voters for such measures.

What happens to education?

The future of education is not marginal to the success or failure of a united Ireland. It matters greatly, of course, to individual and collective quality of life. But it also goes to the heart of the economic question. Whether Northern Ireland can rise to the Republic's level of productivity – and therefore whether the Republic has to continue to subsidise its public services – will depend crucially on whether the gap in educational achievement between the two parts of the island can be closed. This is a formidable challenge and one that would demand the creation of a coherent and integrated all-island educational system. That is something the Republic itself has never managed to create.

By 2020, productivity per worker was approximately 40% higher in the Republic than in Northern Ireland.[51] Much of the North's low productivity is caused by a lack of investment, but a major underlying factor is the way its educational system fails so many pupils and then the loss of many of those who do succeed (especially those from a Protestant/unionist background) to universities in Britain and elsewhere, where they then settle permanently.

Based on figures from 2015, Adele Bergin and Seamus McGuinness report that 35% of young people in Northern Ireland (aged from 24 to 30 years) attained only the two lowest levels of schooling (primary and lower secondary), compared with under 11% in the Republic. The rate of early school leaving in the North is approximately twice that in the South.[52] Conversely, just under 40% of Northern Ireland's young people attained the two highest levels of attainment (post-secondary or third level), compared with approximately 60% in Ireland. Just 23% of adults in Northern Ireland have tertiary education while the comparative figure for Ireland is 47%.

Economists Vani Borooah and Colin Knox have written that the 'system of primary and secondary level education in Northern Ireland is, to the outside observer, a structural morass' with 'a bewildering array of schools influenced by the role played by churches in the management and delivery of education'.[53] At post-primary level alone, there are selective and non-selective schools (grammar and secondary schools); co-education and single-sex schools; 'controlled' (in effect Protestant) schools and Catholic-maintained schools; and integrated schools and Irish-medium schools. Just 5% of schools are integrated and just 8% of all pupils attend those schools. Within this morass, boys – and especially boys from working-class Protestant backgrounds – tend to get lost.

For those who do succeed in progressing to third level, higher education institutions in Northern Ireland have an income per student that is 25% less than in England.[54] The effect is a chronic shortage of places – for every 100 applicants in Northern Ireland there are 60 places.

Both because of this and because of cultural and religious ties to Britain, about 30% of Northern Ireland students go to Britain to study. In 2019, over 17,000 young people from Northern Ireland were studying there.[55] Current projections are for these numbers to double by 2030. And, in turn, only 30% of those who leave to study subsequently return to live and work in Northern Ireland.[56] The economic effects of this exodus have long been recognised, but as the Pivotal Public Policy Forum puts it, 'Despite decades of brain drain and wider economic underperformance in Northern Ireland, there are no strategies in place to address educational migration.'[57]

How would these two realities change in a united Ireland? If 'the role played by churches in the management and delivery of education' is central to the fragmented nature of primary and secondary education in the North, which in turn contributes to grossly unequal outcomes, what does the South look like? It has no state system of primary education at all. Of more than 3,000 primary schools nationally, about 2,700 (88.5%) are controlled by the Catholic Church and 6% by Protestant churches.[58] This control is not theoretical: all teaching staff must hold religious certificates and in the developed world only Israel devotes more time to religion in primary school than Ireland does.[59] At second level, about half of secondary schools have a Catholic patron, with the rest of the system split between Protestant, multidenominational, community and technical schools.

In principle, the Republic has been moving towards a system that is less religious-dominated and more suited to its pluralist society. But in practice a mere fifteen Catholic schools have changed from a religious ethos to a multidenominational one over recent years. Even very obvious reforms like moving religious education out of the compulsory school day have not been implemented. This raises the question of how credible it is to imagine that the Republic could create a coherent educational system by joining its own anachronistically religious one to the 'structural morass' of Northern Ireland's.

The strong likelihood is that a united Ireland would end up with a patchwork of school types and a plethora of different qualifications. Jennifer Todd, in an essay for the ARINS project, suggests that, after unification,

> educational establishments and practices in Northern Ireland could continue unchanged, as would those in the south, with differential standards between each part of the island regarding the teaching of Irish, examination systems—GCSE in Northern Ireland if parents so choose, Leaving Certificate in the south—and differential ease of access to universities in Great Britain … Maximally, the ideal would be that all pupils throughout the island have a choice of the international baccalaureate, GCSE or the Leaving Certificate.[60]

This does not sound like the kind of integrated system that could ensure equality of educational outcomes for all pupils.

As for the second critical issue – Northern Ireland's so-called brain drain – there is no good reason to think that Irish unity would make a positive difference. The pull factor of cultural identification with British universities would probably not weaken – it might even strengthen if young people from a Protestant/unionist background felt alienated from a united Ireland. The push factor of the insufficient number of higher education places available within Northern Ireland could, in principle, be addressed by large-scale investment from the new all-island state.

Optimism about the likelihood of such a commitment has to be tempered by the reality that the Republic's own third-level system remains chronically underfunded. Its experience has been one of increasing enrolments on the one side and declining investment on the other. A 2022 analysis by the European Commission identified a funding shortfall of €307 million in the annual budget for the sector. Subsequent increases in funding have mostly been swallowed up by pay increases for staff. Professor Hugh Brady, former president of UCD and now president of Imperial College London, suggested in June 2024 that 'Irish universities still hold on to top Irish school leaver talent and do a great job with limited resources but, comparatively speaking, the quality of experience is slipping and is only going to get worse over time.'[61]

What would have to change over time in a united Ireland would be the level of public investment in third-level education. But the other costs of unification are likely instead to lead to a weakening of such investment. One does not need to have a PhD to realise that these sums do not add up.

Conclusion

No one could or should rule out the possibility of a united Ireland at some point in the future. It is recognised in law as a legitimate aspiration, and Britain is committed to facilitating it if it is shown to be the wish of a majority of people in Northern Ireland. It has an emotional resonance for most people in the South, and their desire to see it happen is sincere.

But there is an enormous gap between wishing and doing. At the level of government, the Republic is still struggling to catch up with decades of underdevelopment in housing, healthcare, childcare, public transport, infrastructure and social services of every kind. It is also currently incapable of meeting its legal commitments on climate change and the creation of a carbon-free economy. It is simply fanciful to imagine that such a creaking system is capable of managing, in addition, all the immense practical problems that unification would bring.

At the level of civil society, there is simply no evidence that most people in the South have given any real thought to what unification would mean. This is why support for it falls dramatically when almost any real-life qualification – from paying higher taxes to changing the national anthem – is attached to it. The more real it becomes, the more reluctant people seem to be to turn the aspirational into the actual. To adapt T.S. Eliot, Irish idealism cannot bear too much reality.

Before the question of a united Ireland can be considered as a practical proposition, both jurisdictions have a long way to travel.

Fintan O'Toole

The North has to achieve a much greater degree of genuine reconciliation than is evident so far. There cannot be an Irish 'us' when society is still so divided between 'us' and 'them'. The South, meanwhile, has to do an awful lot more nation-building before it can so radically redefine its nationhood. It cannot hope to integrate crucial aspects of its public life like health, welfare and education with the North before it is even capable of integrating them in its own jurisdiction. Bluntly, unification – if it is not to be chaotic, costly and potentially violent – demands a much more robust and effective Southern state than the one that currently exists. When there is a more settled North and a stronger South, unification may become feasible. Before then, it must remain in the realm of vague possibilities.

2.
The case <u>for</u> a united Ireland

SAM McBRIDE

A venerable idea

There was a time, before anyone now alive had breath in their nostrils, when a united Ireland wasn't a controversial concept. That Ireland should be a single political unit was as self-evident to the island's inhabitants as the territorial integrity of Iceland or Australia.

That agreement masked profound differences. Unionists wanted Ireland united under the control of Westminster, nationalists wanted devolved autonomy within the British Empire, while republicans wanted to sever ties with Britain. It was because of the irreconcilability of these competing visions that partition was implemented in 1921. Yet few of those who now defend partition would have done so had they been alive prior to the First World War.

The division of the island into two jurisdictions – and the particular border chosen – was not the product of centuries of careful thought, but a desperate attempt to stave off calamitous civil war. In doing so, the new international frontier rent asunder communities and even individual farms. It destroyed centuries-old natural hinterlands and arbitrarily divided the historic province of Ulster.

Debating the wisdom of that decision is academically stimulating but ultimately of limited benefit in terms of deciding what we in our age should do in what is a dramatically different world. The British Empire has gone, the question over whether Irish men and women could run their own affairs[1] has been decisively settled, the old religious fears of the early twentieth century seem increasingly archaic, and the idea of devolution – once known as Home Rule – is so uncontroversial that the vast majority of unionists as well as nationalists support it. As Wallace Thompson, an evangelical Protestant who was a founding member of the Democratic Unionist Party (DUP) and a close associate of Ian Paisley, reflected in 2021, the Protestants who had fought at the Somme were fighting 'for an Empire which is gone, for a nation which was essentially Protestant in its essence which is gone, and against absorption into an Irish Catholic state which is gone. Much of what our forefathers were fighting for and against has gone.'[2]

Whether we celebrate or mourn the fact that those factors have irrevocably altered, the world we inhabit has changed utterly from that of our ancestors.

What has not changed is the straightforward geographical logic of an island being governed as one. Generally, where islands are divided – in places like Cyprus, Timor and New Guinea – that is to their detriment. If we were the first people arriving into Ireland, the most obvious thought would be to organise the island's affairs on the basis that it is a single unit where one region necessarily impacts on its neighbouring regions.

Some of those once violently hostile to Irish unity are now returning to their ancestral understanding of the island's essential unity, even if in very different circumstances. Referring to Ireland as a single entity, a former loyalist paramilitary recently told me: 'It's a natural way for this island to be.' That individual is for now atypical among his peers, but the logic that informs his new thinking is straightforward.

Divided, yet indivisible

The depth of the divisions on this island are so well understood that they often obscure how much remains undivided. The labels 'Catholic' and 'Protestant' or 'unionist' and 'nationalist' do not come close to the experiences of people truly cut off from each other, such as in apartheid South Africa, the segregated southern US states, or the Jewish–Muslim divide in Israel and Palestine.

As the English anthropologist Anthony Buckley observed in 1982, outside 'very limited and specific exceptions, the cultural heritage for the Catholic is likely to be much the same as that of a Protestant of the same social class living in the same geographical area. There are no distinctively Protestant or Catholic dialects, nor agricultural practices, nor housetypes, nor pottery techniques, nor styles of cooking. Family life is much the same on both sides, as indeed is the broader social morality.'[3]

More than four decades later, this is even more true as a growing section of the population holds more lightly to their political or religious persuasions and the end of the Troubles has allowed for more relaxed cross-community mixing. We see this in how changing social attitudes to issues such as homosexuality and abortion have been broadly similar across the sectarian divide.

While for many people national identity is deeply held, it is not frozen forever for everyone. In Professor Richard Rose's seminal 1968 survey of attitudes in Northern Ireland, he found just 39% of Protestants described themselves as British (20% said Irish, 32% Ulster). Just three in four Catholics described themselves as exclusively Irish (15% said British). A decade later, the Troubles had changed things dramatically: by then, 67% of Protestants said they were British. Today the figure is almost identical.[4]

What this shows is that change even in something as fundamental as how someone voluntarily self-identifies can be dramatic, and sudden. Some unionists would continue to see themselves as solely British after Irish unity, but the evidence does not support the thesis that this would be universal or unchangeable.

The paradoxes of history

In two of the most defining moments of the modern era, northern Protestants managed to precipitate that which they'd sought to prevent – but quickly came to cleave to what they had until recently opposed.

In 1798, the United Irishmen took up arms against what they saw as a despotic system of English control over Ireland. Radical Protestants – among them William Drennan, Theobald Wolfe Tone and Henry Joy McCracken – united with Catholics in a daring effort, in Tone's words, 'to substitute the common name of Irishman in place of the denomination of Protestant, Catholic and Dissenter'. After their military defeat, Britain decided that new constitutional architecture was necessary. Two years later, the Act of Union was passed, influenced by the sectarian slaughter set off by what had been radical Presbyterian idealism. A rebellion intended to unite had divided. An effort to break British rule had strengthened it.

Likewise, in 1921, Edward Carson and James Craig's threat in very different circumstances to take up arms against His Majesty's forces precipitated the sundering of the island they'd wanted to retain intact within the Union, and the brutal abandonment of their allies not only across the rest of the island, but even in three of Ulster's counties. Yet within a few years, this new jurisdiction in which unionists had guaranteed dominance would be shaped by them into something they cherished, with its iconography most grandly encapsulated in the Stormont parliament set atop a hill overlooking Northern Ireland's capital.

Today it is the idealism of 1798 that is widely accepted across the broad sweep of nationalist thinking. No one is now wanting to create a Catholic state in which the Protestant faith would be repressed. No one is advocating a country in which any sect should face discrimination. The imagination of Tone and Drennan has broadened to encompass new migrant communities, a plethora of faiths, multiple sexualities and a broad acceptance of the right of the individual to live their life in freedom according to the dictates of their conscience.

If unity comes, it will be the triumph of that broad-minded vision of what Ireland should be, not the insular, sectarian vision that so many northern Protestants have feared for so long.

Southern indifference

Despite what would become its rhetorical claim on the North in Bunreacht na hÉireann and periodic provocative verbal jousts by politicians, the South quickly came to accept partition. The Irish Republican Army (IRA) was largely forced out of business, the Free State's Defence Forces weren't marshalled for a military assault, and while small gestures towards some possibility of future unity were made, the state's priority was survival – not just for itself, but quite literally for its people.

In his memoir on the long shadow of the Irish Civil War, the war correspondent Fergal Keane pondered why his nationalist ancestors in Listowel had fought for the IRA but ultimately accepted partition. The answer was partly about geography: Ulster had always been a long way from Kerry or Cork, and from Dublin for that matter. It was also religious, cultural and economic: Ulster's massive Protestant population, its sectarian murder gangs, the mills and the Belfast shipyard represented a fundamentally different world to a largely agrarian, Catholic and more settled Ireland.

Keane observed that his ancestors 'did not go to war to capture Belfast and impose Gaelic Catholic supremacy on the entire island of Ireland, but to be masters in their own place, believing they might build a more prosperous happy country outside the British Empire'.[5]

That attitude endured for decades. In 1961, a dismayed IRA issued a statement in which it said weapons had been dumped and there would be an 'end to the resistance campaign', chiefly because of 'the attitude of the general public whose minds have been deliberately distracted from the supreme issue facing the Irish people – the unity and freedom of Ireland'.[6]

When the idiosyncratic Waterford travel writer Dervla Murphy travelled around Northern Ireland on a bicycle in 1976, she marvelled at how far it was from her previous life, envying those who in border counties had at least some contact with Northern Protestants: 'South of the Dublin–Galway line there is little sense of personal involvement with Northern Ireland; it seems much further away than Britain, where so many people have lived and worked, or even than the USA.'[7]

All of this was explicable, and maybe even forgivable. But it stank of hypocrisy. This was a state that claimed to be committed to reuniting the island's territory. Its political parties proclaimed that as their top goal. Yet for decades they consciously did precious little about it. It was too awkward to take the sort of radical action – from opening up the economy to ending the Church's domination of public life – that might have prepared the ground for a gradual rapprochement with unionists, who instead saw some of their worst fears fulfilled.

This attitude also made it easier for grossly sectarian behaviour to flourish in Northern Ireland. It wasn't just that Catholics faced discrimination in jobs or housing, but that they were shut out of the one vehicle to political power. Although there had been a handful of Catholics in the Unionist Party at the time of partition, by 1959 there was a furious backlash when the chairman of the party's standing committee, Sir Clarence Graham, along with the attorney general, Brian Maginess, suggested that Catholics should be able to join the party and even stand as candidates.[8]

Sir George Clark, the unionist senator and Orange Order Grand Master, rebuked Graham, making clear that the Order – which then formally sat on the ruling Ulster Unionist Council – would never accept Catholics in the party's membership. Lord Brookeborough, the prime minister of Northern Ireland, and many others echoed this stance.

This meant that Catholics were being formally excluded from the one political route to real power. Even if they supported the Union, even if they put up with the bigotry that enveloped them, and even if they agreed with every unionist policy, they were being told that purely on the basis of their faith they were ineligible.

Those responsible for this were unionists. But the Republic's partitionist approach meant there was little serious effort to help those cut adrift of the new state by securing reunification. Not only did this abandonment hurt Northern nationalists, it arguably even hurt unionists because it enabled them to perpetuate a system of government that became ever more absurd as the twentieth century progressed, ultimately collapsing amid the slaughter of the Troubles.

Southern voters today who are mentally distanced from Northern Ireland, who perhaps have never crossed the border and who care little about whether Ireland is united, bear a particular responsibility to consider these matters seriously. How would they feel if Cork and Kerry and Limerick and Waterford had been abandoned in this way and Northern nationalists walked past on the other side of the road?

A longstanding British belief in Irish unity

Sir Winston Churchill long regarded partition as an unfortunate but temporary aberration from Ireland's natural state – even if the wartime prime minister desired unity within the British Empire, something now long gone.

Three years after the end of the Second World War, the man who would later be voted the greatest Briton of all time told the Commons: 'It seemed to me that the passage of time might lead to the unity of Ireland itself in the only way in which that unity can be achieved, namely, by a union of Irish hearts. There can, of course, be no question of coercing Ulster, but if she were wooed and won of her own free will and consent I, personally, would regard such an event as a blessing for the whole of the British Empire and also for the civilised world.'[9]

By the late 1960s, Prime Minister Harold Wilson similarly believed that a united Ireland was the only viable long-term solution to Northern Ireland's problems – a view shared by the chancellor, home secretary, foreign secretary and defence secretary. The Irish government panicked, fearing a sudden, chaotic British withdrawal, while British civil servants warned that the British presence was necessary to prevent full-blown civil war.[10]

The Union has endured, and in some regards it has worked. The succession of bloody battles on the island of Britain has settled into centuries of deeply embedded peace. Even where English, Scottish or Welsh nationalists want to break up the Union, those who wish to use violence to do so have long been at the margins of the margin.

But in Ireland the Union has failed to deliver sustained peace and justice. Its promises of rapid Catholic emancipation were abandoned when George III refused to give his approval – and then the situation grew darker. For many Irish people, the independence movement stemmed from the Famine of the mid-nineteenth century. Wealthy Britain's failure to act humanely in the gravest crisis the island had ever seen demonstrated that self-determination was a matter of life and death.

The case for a united Ireland

As the conservative British writer Ferdinand Mount observed: 'England's indifference to the miseries of the Famine offers the most conspicuous and shameful proof of how little the Union touched English hearts, and of how little purchase Irish MPs [Members of Parliament] had at Westminster until the last decades of the nineteenth century, when they enjoyed the balance of power.'[11]

In the tempests of the ages, Ireland's bloody history is not unique. But it involved brutality and wilful ignorance of what was happening. Ireland was not some far-off colony, but just a few miles across the sea and a land known well to powerful British families from centuries of property ownership, trade, intermarriage and military service.

Cancerous sectarianism led to both active and passive depravity. In the late nineteenth century, the Rev. W.M. O'Hanlon found living conditions in the largely Catholic area of Smithfield in Belfast to be 'dangerous and perishing'. Conveying the rank poverty of the squalid conditions, he described how as many as seven people would live in a single room with no glass in the windows. The only heat was the huddling together of human bodies against the intruding elements. Food was scarce, as was work. The unskilled men were often unemployed; the women and girls worked on bundles of linen for which they were paid pennies.[12]

Yet this was the era in which Belfast was booming. Some of its most iconic architecture was built on the backs of the wretched. There might not have been slavery in Belfast, but there was obscene injustice.

By 1891, Catholics made up 26% of Belfast's population. The following year a House of Commons report found that on four key city bodies – the Harbour Board, City Corporation, Water Commissioners and Poor Law Board – Protestants held 98% of the positions.[13]

However, the Union's failures have not just been towards Catholics or nationalists, but also towards unionists. On innumerable occasions, unionism has been left lamenting betrayal by Britain. The unionist historian Antony Alcock referred in 1994 to 'the bafflement and frustration of a community which sees its history as one of defending Britain and British interests, yet has felt utterly rejected by the nation that created it'.[14]

To this day, the House of Commons almost invariably empties for Northern Ireland business. Not a single British national newspaper has a full-time correspondent in Belfast and rarely does even dramatic Northern Ireland news make their front pages unless – as with Brexit – it's also crucial to Britain. Northern Ireland has developed as a place apart: legally British, but culturally, politically and economically remote.

There is a plaintive quality to how unionism's leaders have raged against the betrayals of the nation they cherish. The disappointments have been relentless, and go back to the very start. As partition came in, Lord Carson, the eloquent leader of Ulster's unionists, bitterly addressed the House of Lords in 1921: 'But why is all this attack made upon Ulster? What has Ulster done? I will tell you what Ulster has done. She has stuck too well to you, and you believe that because she is loyal you can kick her as you like.'[15]

More than six decades later, a successor of Carson, Jim Molyneaux, told the House of Commons: 'Some honourable members who represent constituencies in Great Britain can, if they wish, continue to regard Northern Ireland as a faraway province of which they know little and care even less. They may find it tempting to rush to the tape machine to check the latest cricket scores and to ignore the paragraph reporting the murder of two Ulster policemen.'[16]

An enduring Northern Ireland

Many unionists – and many Southerners – assume that a united Ireland would mean the end of Northern Ireland. The breaking of the British link would be traumatic enough for unionists. Losing the place their forebears built and which they have come to love would be a psychological blow for many of them.

Yet there is every reason to believe that Northern Ireland could continue after Irish unity. Increasingly, informed thinking in politics and academia has seriously considered the continuation of Northern Ireland whereby the Good Friday Agreement is inverted, with Dublin replacing the roles currently carried out by London but with significant power residing in Belfast. In such a situation, the Stormont administration would continue, the institutions of Northern Irish life such as the PSNI and the Northern Ireland civil service would remain, and perhaps even the Northern Ireland football team.

Instead of sending MPs to Westminster, Northern Ireland would send TDs (*Teachta Dála*; equivalent of MP) to the Dáil, and instead of London sending a big cheque for Stormont to spend, the big cheque would come from Dublin. The currency would change, as would the postal service, the TV licence and other national aspects of life. But what remained would entail considerable familiarity. This arrangement could last indefinitely, if it worked – or could be a transitional period in which incremental change took place.

Taoiseach Micheál Martin said in 2017 that a future united Ireland would 'hold fast to the principles enshrined in the Good Friday Agreement' and 'that could mean in a future united Ireland you would still have a Northern Executive and a Northern Assembly'.[17] In some ways, this is consistent with a section of longstanding Southern political opinion. As far back as 1959, Seán Lemass told the Oxford Union that Stormont – then a very different place with no power-sharing – would stay if there was a united Ireland.[18] Even further back, the Irish Constitution provided for regional assemblies[19] – a clear preparation for the possibility of keeping Stormont even at a time when that involved de facto one-party rule.

It's true that this would mean retaining some of the most dysfunctional elements of Northern Ireland, but there would be much greater oversight of the devolved institutions because Dublin has a far greater stake in this than London. Infrastructure could be planned on an all-island basis without the complexity of navigating an international frontier while the North should benefit from the overspill of the vast Southern economy. By being plugged into the Irish civil service, Stormont's bureaucrats would be overseen far more closely than at present.

There are counterarguments to this, most cogently set out by Professor Brendan O'Leary. Could Northern TDs vote on Southern issues in the Dáil? If not, Northern TDs would be second-class parliamentarians and so have less value in forming governing coalitions. Could a Northern TD fulfil the equivalent role of secretary of state? As O'Leary observes, some ways of ensuring Northern access to national executive power – such as a rule that the taoiseach be a Southerner and the tánaiste a Northerner – 'fit poorly with the idea of a common citizenship in a united Ireland'.[20] These constitutional difficulties would be combined with the inescapable practical problem that many of the efficiencies Irish unity could bring would be lost, replicating service after service in both jurisdictions.

If a unitary state is not going to be a return to anything like de Valera's Ireland, then even some non-nationalists who are open to unity think that as much of the dysfunctionality of Northern Ireland as possible should be swept away as soon as possible. To delay, they believe, means simply prolonging the problems. Similarly, the more separate Northern Ireland is kept, the greater the potential resentment of Southerners if for decades they are sending massive subsidies to the north-east while accepting what may be other painful compromises. There are other options, such as a federal Ireland based on the historic four provinces, which would decentralise power closer to the population.

It is difficult now to say precisely what form unity might take when nationalism has not yet agreed on a preferred option. Yet the very fact of this debate speaks to the possibilities inherent in this moment: very little has yet been decided, and those who engage now have considerable opportunities to shape what could become a new country.

Regardless of the shape that unity might take, in some senses Northern Ireland will always exist; there is now a regional identity that cannot be wholly erased at the stroke of a legislator's pen – at least for many decades. There are things Northern Ireland's people will always share, regardless of the constitutional situation. For Northerners, their next-door neighbour will still be their next-door neighbour after unity; their children will still go to the local school; their family will still live in the locality. They might not want unity, but if it comes it will not be a fundamental rupture of everything they know.

A pluralist state for a pluralist people

In 1989, John Hume told an interviewer: 'The unionist people have a long and strong tradition in Ireland. They have a rich Protestant heritage and a great pride in their tradition. They have pride in their service to the Crown, pride in their contribution to the United States, in their spirit of industry and achievement, in their work ethic and in their faith.' Speaking as the Troubles raged, the towering leader of twentieth-century Irish nationalism said that the simple yet fundamental question facing society was 'How do we share this island piece of earth together, in a manner that gives supremacy to none?'[21]

Some 36 years later, with Ireland economically prosperous and with the Catholic Church more powerless than any time since the Act of Union, there is evidence of tangible change of the sort that means sharing this piece of earth without bloodshed is more possible than at any point since partition. If the Republic ever was a 'pathetic, sectarian, mono-ethnic, monocultural State', as David Trimble controversially described it in 2002, those days are long gone.[22]

Hume spoke of Irishness as something that entailed 'extraordinary diversity – for a small island, we are probably one of the most diverse peoples in the world'. He referred to 'the streams that made up Ireland – the Celts, the Normans, the English, the Scots'.[23] Even Ireland's patron saint came from Britain.

Modern Ireland is so much more diverse, ethnically, culturally, socially and religiously.

For some people, there is justice in Irish unity; it is about righting the wrongs of antiquity. This has the potential to manifest itself in ugly acts of retribution or discrimination. Yet the Irish nation of today is one in which the dominant thinking focuses on accommodation and looking forward.

More than 20% of the population was born outside the island[24] – and that figure will climb due to a still-falling birthrate. If those people can be welcomed – as they have been by the great bulk of the population – then so can people whose ancestors have lived here for hundreds of years. Newcomers will continue to dilute the residual historic hostility to unionism; they have no ancient quarrel with those whose ancestors may have come here centuries ago. Indeed, the slur 'planter', which is still used by some republicans today, should become increasingly socially unacceptable as its implication of two-tier Irishness for migrants is understood.

There are many unionists who remain sceptical of claims that they'd be well treated in a united Ireland. Far from being unreasonable, those fears are quite logical. If they were 95% sure they wouldn't face discrimination, even a 5% chance that they'd be targeted because of their religion or politics is an enormous risk.

Yet one man is the embodiment of how Ireland has dramatically demonstrated by actions rather than words that the old 'Home Rule is Rome rule' mentality is dead and buried. His name is Drew Harris, the Garda commissioner at the time of writing.

He isn't just a Northern Protestant. He's a former Royal Ulster Constabulary (RUC) officer – indeed, the former RUC Special Branch officer who liaised with MI5. Yet the Irish government trusted this man to protect its national security. There was some grumbling from republicans when he was appointed in 2018, but it never went anywhere – and he was reappointed for a second term.

There was no sense that this was being done to make a political point, far less to draw the lesson from it that I am drawing. No state gives such a sensitive post to someone to tick a diversity box. He was, quite simply, judged to be the best person for the job of rescuing a police service weighed down with scandal and incompetence.

The new state would have enormous self-interest in keeping unionists happy. If it didn't, many of them might leave, taking their skills to Britain or elsewhere. Retaining this talent pool would provide a self-interested incentive to treat unionists well.

The case for a united Ireland

A wise nationalist leadership would kill unionists with kindness. After centuries of enmity, words can be discarded but far harder to dismiss are tangible offerings – financial investment in unionist areas, gestures by nationalist leaders, and changing national symbols to show the seriousness of the commitment to a truly new dispensation.

There are those like former Northern Ireland first minister Arlene Foster who have said they would leave if there was a united Ireland. Far more numerous are those who would stay. Unless faced with intolerable conditions, most unionists would adopt the view of the Belfast poet John Hewitt that 'this is our country and nowhere else/and we shall not be outcast on the world'.[25]

What is now being offered by the South to the North is so substantial that it would have shocked past generations. In 1974, the Ulster Volunteer Force (UVF) leadership said:

> Our basic objective is to preserve our Protestant liberties and traditions and our British way of life. By that we don't mean the preservation of the link with Britain but of those traditions of religious and civil freedoms which have characterised British democracy. When we talk of the preservation of our Protestant traditions and liberties we simply mean that we want to ensure that we are able to worship God in the manner of our choice and not according to the ordinance or dictate of any outside organisations such as the Catholic Church.[26]

Setting aside the grotesque hypocrisy of an organisation involved in the cold-blooded butchery of the innocent talking about its desire to worship God, this was a strikingly pragmatic statement: even at the height of the Troubles, the UVF was here accepting that if civil and religious liberty could be guaranteed, it was open to radical thinking. Everything the UVF then demanded has been met, and then some.

Not only is Ireland a nation with a high regard for individual freedom, democracy and the rule of law, it is brimming with wealth. Whereas in 1974 amalgamation with the South would have meant poverty, now it means prosperity.

When viewed in the arc of even living history, the distance travelled is immense. Many of those who hold out against what is now on offer do so from a position of ignorance, either of what Ireland now is or of what some of their unionist ancestors would once have accepted.

The warm welcomes Ireland has shown to the late Queen Elizabeth II and to King Charles III signify a conclusive burying of the hatchet between almost all of nationalism and the Royal Family. Sinn Féin's decision to attend not only the state funeral of the late queen but then also the coronation of the new king was an astonishing move for any republican party, let alone one with Sinn Féin's history.

Similarly, the marking of the centenary of the Easter Rising demonstrated the Republic's maturity. The 2016 Republic was a state far more confident and self-reflective than had been the case 50 years previously, enabling it to commemorate the British soldiers and the Irish policemen whom the 1916 rebels killed, even if in the tense Brexit-era years that followed there would be pushback against such magnanimity. A former taoiseach, John Bruton, felt able to publicly denounce the moral choices of the rebels.[27]

A shoreless ocean of possibility

Almost immediately after unity, there would be small simplifications such as an end to having to navigate two currencies and an end to phone signal roaming at the border. But these would merely represent the foothills of the potential benefits.

A lower corporation tax rate for the whole island would drastically increase foreign investment in the north-east, particularly due to lower wage costs, cheaper property and good universities. There would be immediate gains for tourism. Foreign visitors would no longer worry about changing currency or possible visa implications of crossing an international frontier. The Republic's media would

The case for a united Ireland

benefit from a bigger market and a larger pool of staff, especially if RTÉ subsumed BBC NI (Northern Ireland) into its operations.

It would involve increased support for the arts. Ireland is a cultural superpower with global influence in music, books and film. Investment in the arts in Northern Ireland sits at £5.44 per person – in the Republic it's almost five times higher.[28]

For those north of the border, unity would mean a more democratic say in their lives. They would constitute around 25% of the population, whereas in the UK they're less than 3%. At present, Northern Irish voters can't even vote for MPs who might be part of the government in London. The Conservatives stand token candidates who flop, while Labour bans its members from standing at all.

Irish unity would allow Northern Irish voters, whether left-wing or right-wing, socially liberal or conservative, environmentalist or corporatist, to have a more direct say in how they are governed. Brexit demonstrated the need for Northern Ireland to control its own affairs. Indeed, it shows the risks to the entire island of decisions impacting six Irish counties but taken by voters in England.

England's control is unassailable: it holds 54% of the UK's land, more than 80% of its voters, and the lion's share of money. Even within England, it is London that has the greatest control of finance, culture, media and the arts.

Unity would also mean sweeping away the monarchy, an antiquated system of embedded inequality that has produced some fine unifying figures such as Queen Elizabeth II but also the loathsome Prince Andrew – who could still be king if those ahead of him in the line of succession were to die.

Unity would decisively extinguish the endless debate about Northern Ireland's constitutional future, bringing finality to the question. There would be no return to the Union and so while there would be new debates about culture and language and ensuring those who opposed unity were treated fairly, they would be much closer to real politics as it exists in most democratic countries. All of that energy could be spent on trying to resolve far more practical problems.

Better for your health

For decades, even plenty of hard-headed Northern nationalists have supported the Union in the short term for one principal reason: the NHS. Yet it has increasingly become a mirage. For many people in Northern Ireland, their right to be seen by a doctor is unenforceable, and therefore meaningless.

Unionists present the NHS as the jewel in the crown of the Union. Yet they have presided over its decimation, showing no urgency about repairing that which they hope will persuade open-minded voters to pragmatically back the Union.

In Northern Ireland, the NHS has become an elaborate fiction. It promises to treat everyone free at the point of need, but can't. Waiting lists are so long that in some cases people have no realistic prospect of being treated on the NHS before they are dead. Some people wait a decade for a hip replacement. Even if that eventually comes, it entails the unquantifiable suffering of a decade in agony in order to get treated 'free'.[29]

Increasingly there is a two-tier Northern health system: the rich and moderately well off have private health insurance or pay for treatment as they need it, while the poor are left to live in agony and die before their time. As those with influence in society are lifted out of the NHS system, so the incentives for its urgent reform are reduced. The poor might be dying and that might be preventable, but their voices will grow ever fainter.

The understandable love for what the NHS represents embodies devotion to a glorious ideal, but one that is years out of touch with reality. In 2022, a refugee fleeing the Ukraine war came to Northern Ireland and then needed an urgent operation. The waiting list was so long that they considered returning to Ukraine for treatment.[30] No refugee who has travelled 1,500 miles from a hellish war zone would consider returning there if the NHS was functioning even remotely close to what its founders intended.

This represents monstrous injustice to the poor, yet Stormont has made it worse. Where is the hope for Northern Ireland when the only way it can be credibly governed is by Stormont, but that

SO I FIGURED IF I JOIN THE WAITING LIST NOW I MIGHT BE ABLE TO GET A HIP REPLACEMENT ON TIME

institution makes the most life-and-death aspect of its citizens' lives worse? The power-sharing system has incentivised populism, whereby difficult but necessary decisions such as the centralisation of key services have for decades been avoided. Now unplanned reform is happening as parts of the system collapse.

Data analyst Peter Donaghy calculated in 2023 that almost 38% of people on NHS waiting lists in Northern Ireland have been waiting for more than two years, compared with 0.016% in England. But he explained that in fact it's even worse, because 'the different methodologies used for statistics in England and Northern Ireland mean that this comparison actually flatters Northern Ireland'.[31]

Analysis by the think-tank Pivotal just before the Covid-19 pandemic showed that 120,201 people in Northern Ireland were waiting more than a year for treatment – while in England and Wales the figure was just 1,154. Even if Northern Ireland had the same population as England and Wales, that would be astonishing evidence of failure, but Northern Ireland's population is just over 3% that of England and Wales.

This is no longer a truly national health service. Northern Ireland is now drastically beyond what people in Britain would recognise as a crisis; it is operating to wholly incomparable expectations of the treatment the NHS should provide. The consequences are grim. Almost 62% of Northern Irish people diagnosed with a less survivable cancer will be dead within a year – the worst survival rates in the UK.[32]

The most alarming thing about this is that cancer care is one of the few health services that have been centralised in centres of expertise. Yet wider failures in the system such as struggling to get an appointment with a family doctor undo that progress.

The Southern system – a confused and confusing mixture of public and private – is deeply flawed, yet its outcomes are now clearly better in many areas. For every 1,000 people in 2021, there were four active doctors in the Republic; in Northern Ireland the figure was just 3.6.[33] More up-to-date comparable data are difficult to find – a regular problem in comparing the two parts of the

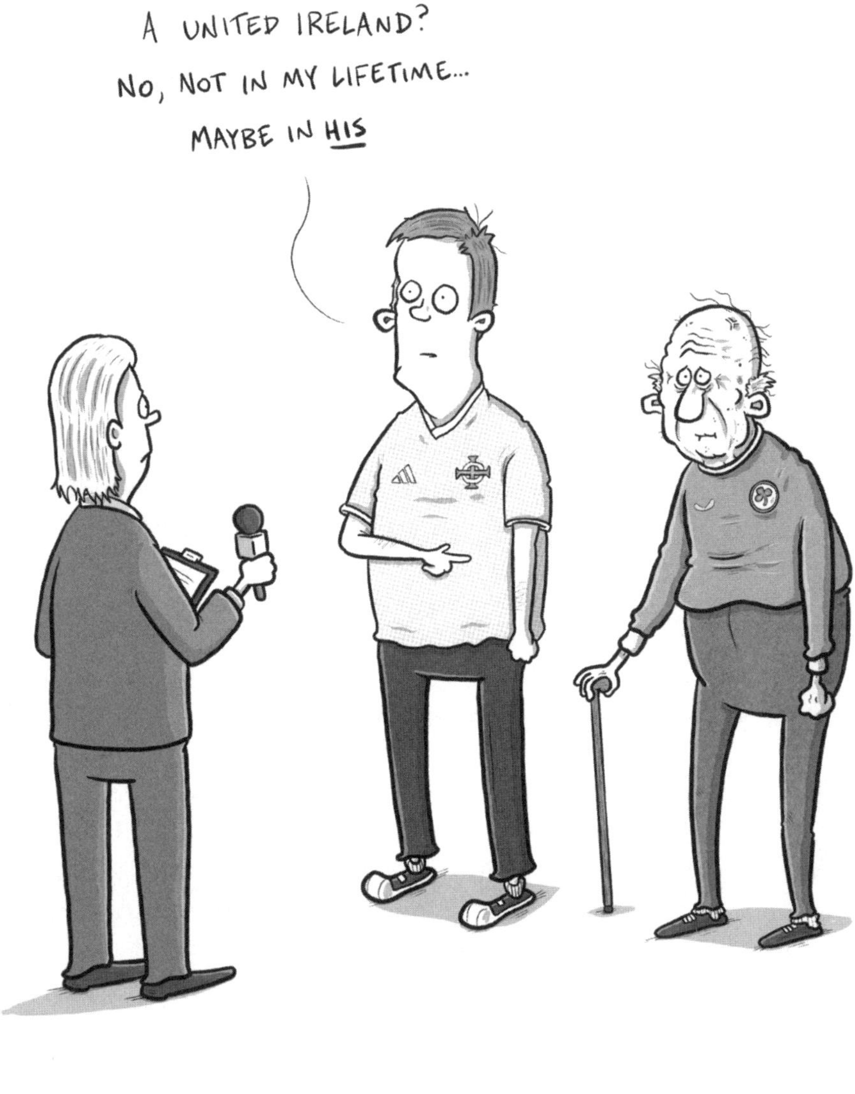
A UNITED IRELAND?
NO, NOT IN MY LIFETIME...
MAYBE IN HIS

island, due to different data collection, categorisation and publication regimes.

But since 2021, the crisis in the Northern Ireland NHS[34] has deepened while Ireland has invested more in health, meaning that the situation is almost certainly more unbalanced today.

In 2024, Professor Austin Smyth, an economist, and two former senior members of the Northern Ireland Audit Office, Sean McKay and Alan Orme, analysed how the island's two health systems had coped with the pandemic. They found significantly higher infection rates and death rates in the North; if the Northern experience had been replicated in the South, it would have experienced up to 1,800 more deaths.[35] They found that overall hospital waiting lists in Northern Ireland were twice as long as in the Republic; lists of those waiting more than a year were four times longer in the North. Yet Northern Ireland spends more per person on health than any other UK nation.

It is true that Northern Ireland had a faster roll-out of the Covid-19 vaccine due to being part of the UK and that there was a uniquely unserious prime minister in office at the time, whose flippancy cost lives. But even allowing for these factors, such research is sobering; this is a health system that has profound structural problems.

In a future border poll, it will be possible for each side to selectively quote statistics for various treatments that have better or worse outcomes on one side of the border or the other. This is legitimate, but confusing – and confusion can be dangerously misleading.

What is beyond debate is that those in the Republic live longer. This is partly explained by better education and greater wealth, but it is scarcely credible that an inferior health system could keep people alive for longer. For a decade, life expectancy in the South has surpassed that in the North. Northern Ireland's life expectancy is 80.6 years; the Republic's is 83.1.[36]

This is not only about the decline of the NHS; it was happening even after Labour pumped record sums into the UK's health system at the start of the century. But as the NHS crumbles, this divide is almost certain to get starker. Medics are leaving Northern Ireland

Life expectancy at one year old and under

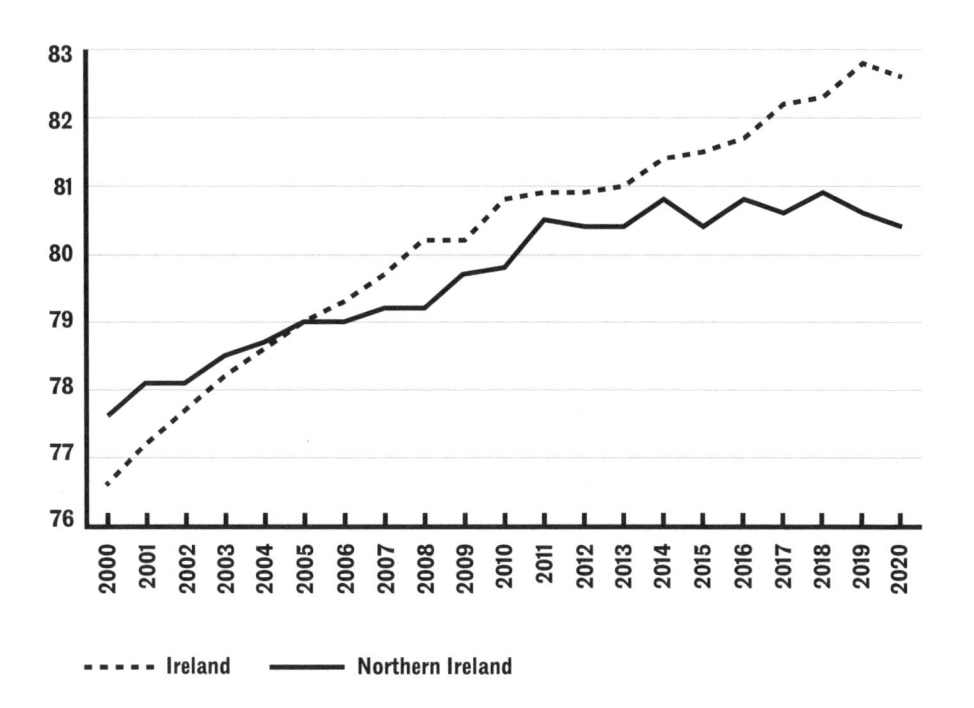

[Chart showing life expectancy from 2000 to 2020 for Ireland (dashed line) and Northern Ireland (solid line). Ireland rises from ~76.5 in 2000 to ~82.7 by 2019. Northern Ireland rises from ~78 in 2000 to ~80.4 by 2020.]

- - - - - Ireland   ——— Northern Ireland

Source: Eurostat, life expectancy by age, sex and NUTS 2 region.

because they can earn far more just a few miles down the road. Economics ultimately drives much of modern life. With deeper pockets, when the two jurisdictions both need doctors, it's the Republic that can make the best offer.

On this basis, Irish unity would quite literally be good for your health if you live in Northern Ireland. And yet, it's likely to benefit Southerners too. Because of the residual affection for the NHS in Northern Ireland, it is highly likely that Sláintecare will be extended to at least go much further towards an NHS-style system by the time a border poll is held. Winning such a referendum without such an offering would be exceptionally difficult.

That would mean benefits for Southerners through a simplified state system in which they pay less for basic medical care.

A stark educational divide

International rankings show that the Republic has not only a better education system than Northern Ireland, but a more egalitarian one. While by global standards Northern Ireland's education system is good, only its very top grammars produce better results than the Republic's – and even there the difference is now small. The Republic has the ninth-best post-primary education system in the world – and the second-best at reading, according to the Programme for International Student Assessment (PISA).[37] Fewer pupils are left behind educationally in the Republic – a critical ingredient for a successful society.[38] The number of young people leaving education early in Northern Ireland is double that of the Republic.[39] The Republic has substantially lower university fees and a culture that appreciates the central value of education – both as a civilising force and as a key to economic progress.

Even the DUP's Paul Givan, now Stormont's education minister, accepts that there are deep problems in Northern Ireland's education system. In more than half of secondary schools, the average proportion of children obtaining the requisite GCSE passes is just 28%. In other secondary schools, it's just 51%. Years of fruitless debate about academic selection for eleven-year-olds, and the inability of Stormont to make a decision due to its system of mutual vetoes, have absorbed most of the energy for deep political thinking about education. The price is being paid by children – especially boys – heading into a job market, and into a life, where they are disadvantaged from the outset.

This isn't just about education. In UNICEF's rankings of countries with the least child poverty, Ireland is the seventh-best state in the rich world; the UK is 37th, behind Romania, Bulgaria and Chile.[40]

The Good Friday Agreement has been remarkably successful at bringing peace to Northern Ireland, but depressingly unsuccessful at bringing good government – or any government at all for years on end. This is a region that has tried majority rule, has tried direct rule, has tried power-sharing – it has even tried

Post-primary education scores

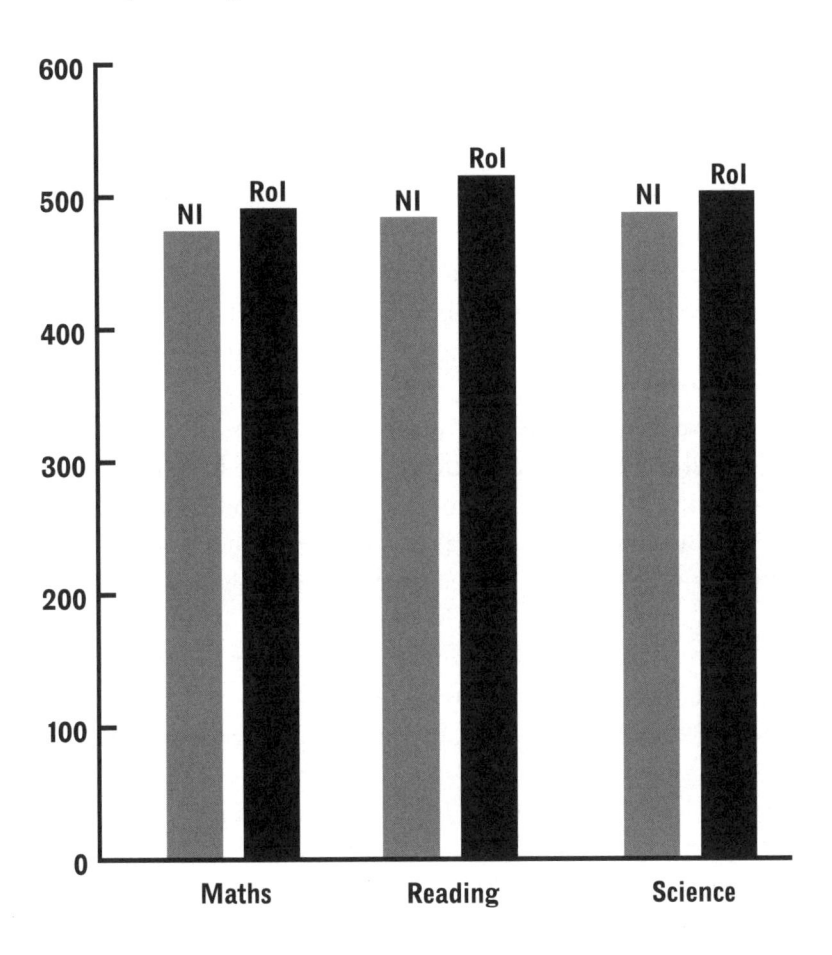

[Bar chart showing PISA 2022 scores for NI and RoI across Maths (NI ~475, RoI ~490), Reading (NI ~485, RoI ~515), and Science (NI ~490, RoI ~505).]

Data from 2022 Programme for International Student Assessment (PISA) for 2022, which benchmarks post-primary education systems around the world.

a quasi-anarchic system of having no government at all. Nothing has reliably worked. There comes a point when the Einsteinian wisdom becomes inescapable: trying the same thing over and over is unlikely to lead to a different result.

Confronting violent bullies

The greatest threat to nationalism winning a border poll, and the greatest threat to the success of a new Ireland, is loyalist violence. This is a threat that cannot be wished away, but must be confronted. As observed by Professor Brendan O'Leary, 'unifying Ireland in referendums must be done carefully to avoid civil war, let alone state collapse'.[41] Yet a rational analysis of the strengths and weaknesses of those who might murder to get their way demonstrates that they have considerable vulnerabilities.

The great fear is that loyalist bombs in the South could persuade Southerners to vote against unity. Recalling his Kerry family's view of the far-off North, Fergal Keane observed that the existing geographical detachment was amplified by the outbreak of the Troubles: 'the effect was to reinforce our desire to be left alone'.[42]

Yet bombs in Dublin or Limerick or Cork would be a massive risk for loyalists. They could galvanise Northern as well as Southern opinion behind the belief that the pro-Union argument had become murderously negative. And it could – as has happened when loyalists attacked Alliance Party offices over the past decade – spectacularly backfire, with voters deciding that in the privacy of the polling booth they will tell the bully boys precisely what they think of them.

In 2021, an umbrella group for loyalist paramilitaries told Irish ministers that they were 'no longer welcome' north of the border. Irish ministers ignored the threat. The following year, a hoax bomb warning targeted Irish minister Simon Coveney during a Belfast visit – but it rebounded on loyalism. As police investigated the hoax, they arrested bungling senior UVF commander Winston Irvine, catching him red-handed with guns.[43] Those who live by the sword don't always die by the sword, but we should be careful not to assume that violence always succeeds.

While a border poll has the potential to be immensely destabilising, it could counterintuitively act as a moderating influence. Committed unionists and nationalists in Northern Ireland are sure to vote for their side; the only votes to be won are the large cohort of the constitutionally undecided – now about 20% of the electorate – who will decide the outcome. This substantial segment of swing voters would have been unthinkable for most of Northern Ireland's history. Yet now the winner will be the side that most effectively speaks to these people. What we know about these voters is that they don't like tribalism, they don't like sectarianism, and they most certainly don't like violence.

Unlike Northern Ireland elections, which are contested within tribal blocs, this plebiscite will involve a structural incentive towards centrist arguments. Even if that fails and a referendum provokes white-hot anger, the strength of loyalist paramilitaries might not be what it seems on paper. The UK's intelligence agencies are known to have heavily infiltrated the UVF, Ulster Defence Association (UDA) and smaller groups. If it is in Britain's strategic interests to ensure a peaceful transfer of sovereignty, it should have significant influence on how those organisations behave or at the very least have good intelligence on what they're up to.

As part of the Five Eyes intelligence network, the UK has access to the world's most sophisticated intelligence-gathering operation. The US, whose companies are heavily exposed to any potential violence, has self-interested reasons to share any knowledge of loyalist attempts to secure arms.

For years the IRA unjustifiably sought to coerce unionists into accepting a united Ireland. For loyalists to seek to coerce nationalists out of supporting a united Ireland would be equally reprehensible. Democracy hinges on the will of the people, not the size of a thug's gun barrel.

As the conservative English philosopher Roger Scruton observed: 'Toleration means being prepared to accept opinions that you intensely dislike. Likewise, democracy means consenting to be governed by people whom you intensely dislike.'[44] The challenge for unionism would be to isolate the murderous in the way that nationalism has isolated dissident republicans. If it worked, that could decisively see the removal of the gun from Irish politics. There would be an illogicality to loyalist violence that would likely push thinking unionists away from supporting it.

Once Britain leaves, it's not coming back. The UK is compelled by its commitments in the Good Friday Agreement to accept the result of a border poll. Only the most deluded unionist could imagine that setting off bombs or shooting Catholics would somehow retrieve what had been lost.

Thus, any insurrection would immediately transgress one of the prerequisites of a just war: it would have no chance of success. Lashing out in rage in such circumstances would be impossible to present even to fellow unionists, much less the wider world, as a reasonable defence of a righteous cause.

In 1996, David Trimble said: 'The reason Sinn Féin exist, and why they resort to terrorism, is because they know they cannot succeed by democratic means.'[45] There was considerable truth in what he said. But to recount those words is to recall the scale of unionist failure since then.

Now, almost all republicans have foresworn violence – and unionist parties have presided over a drastic fall in their own vote. If nationalism, having agreed to wholly constitutional means, should win, the goalposts cannot be moved. To move them not only would be morally wrong but would lead to unionists being shunned by the democratic world.

Only a fool would say that this means violence can't happen. The suspected informants at the top of loyalist paramilitary groups could be swept away in a patriotic rage. Britain could decide for Machiavellian reasons not to do everything it could to bear down on these groups. Heavy infiltration of organisations could create complacency that misses lone wolves.

Of all the potential problems, this one should not be dismissed. But there are reasons to believe that a loyalist insurrection, were it to happen, would be unsuccessful.

What the South gains

The Republic in 2025 is one of the greatest places there has ever been to live in the history of the world. The UN Human

The case for a united Ireland

Development Index, which measures quality of life, rates the Republic as the seventh-best country in the world. The UK is fifteenth – and Northern Ireland is one of the UK's most deprived areas.[46]

It is easier for Southerners to think that unity isn't terribly important because their state is already successful. But its success involves heavy caveats, and enormous risks. Structuring an economy to be dependent on foreign firms' avoidance of tax bills elsewhere involves twin vulnerabilities: that someone else will undercut that offer; and that foreign governments, most significantly the US administration, as is now being seen, will force their companies to pay tax in their jurisdictions. Wisely, Irish governments have been investing billions from this windfall in a sovereign wealth fund, while also pouring money into infrastructure, education and fostering an entrepreneurial culture.

Yet the Republic is the most unequal society among the rich nations of the world.[47] The country's top 10% holds about half its wealth; the bottom 50% of the population holds just 12% of the wealth. This is not just unjust, but unsustainable. History is littered with nations whose gross inequality led to revolution.

Just because Ireland is now laden with gold doesn't mean that will always be so. Even some senior Irish business figures have expressed fears for social solidarity if the gap cannot be bridged between extreme wealth and those unable to even afford a roof over their heads.

Unity provides a rare opportunity to radically reshape the Republic, keeping its best bits while building in the best parts of Northern Ireland. Ultimately, it is up to the public to decide if they want the most radical change – a new unitary state – or more incremental change that involves keeping most of the Republic and Northern Ireland as they are after a transfer of sovereignty from London.

In a united Ireland, the Republic's territory would increase by 20% and its population by more than 35%. Ireland would have a bigger population than Norway, Denmark, Finland or Singapore. That would mean increased influence in the EU and globally.

The problematic concentration of the Republic's population on Dublin could be relieved, with Belfast immediately becoming the state's second city. That would ease pressure on property and infrastructure in the capital. There would be access to cheaper labour and cheaper property in the north-east.

The border regions would most obviously benefit. The north-west of the island has been isolated by poor transport links; rectifying this would help not only Donegal and Derry but the rest of the island.

The creation, for instance, of an Atlantic corridor of motorway and rail could link Londonderry and Limerick, and then on to Cork. Areas now far from most of the population would be brought closer, benefiting business and tourism. There would be a cost to this, of course. But the Republic is now a supremely wealthy country with a sovereign wealth fund that is planned to be at least €100 billion by the mid-2030s. Spending on infrastructure – as the Romans and the Victorians realised – is an investment for decades or centuries into the future.

Infrastructure is the engine of economic development; behind roads, bridges, water and electricity come people and jobs and hitherto unthinkable possibilities.

Placing the border around the entire island would allow Ireland's frontier to be policed more rigorously. People trafficking, drug smuggling and the evasion of the law have been facilitated by a farcical situation where there is an international border on the island that is almost entirely unregulated at the border itself. This has enabled fuel smuggling that has trashed the environment in places like south Armagh, with the toxic sludge left after removing fuel dye being dumped in the countryside. Without a differential taxation rate, this would be instantly eradicated.

Unity would mean a far bigger home market – the market in which it is easiest to trade. It would increase competition in a Southern market where many goods are significantly more expensive than in the UK.

A bigger population would make possible some health procedures not currently feasible in two smaller jurisdictions. There would be countless savings and benefits from the economies of scale inherent to a larger entity.

Unless agreed otherwise, a new country would mean a united football team. Rugby and cricket have shown how a single team can both achieve sporting success while sensitively respecting the diversity of Northern and Southern fans.

But the South would also gain in more intangible ways. Unity would mean reclaiming the wider diversity of the island by reintegrating the dissenting Protestant tradition and the Presbyterian culture of logical debate. America's great melting pot of cultures has demonstrated how the strengths of varied traditions can be harnessed to creative effect. It would be a reimagination of what Ireland is, and what it can be.

Squandered economic potential

When Ireland was partitioned, it was the Northern state that was endowed with immense wealth. As early as 1894, H.O. Lanyon, president of the Belfast Chamber of Commerce, boasted that the length of yarn produced by the city each year amounted to 644,000,000 miles, making a thread that would encircle the world 25,000 times.

By 1912, as the Home Rule crisis deepened and – although still unseen – the First World War loomed, the economy of what is now Northern Ireland was even stronger. It was an industrial leviathan of global proportions now difficult to comprehend.

The historian Jonathan Bardon recalled:

> At the beginning of the twentieth century Belfast was, after London and Liverpool, the port of third importance in the United Kingdom, then the greatest trading state on earth; and in 1912 it had the world's biggest linen mill, ropeworks, tobacco factory, spiral-guided gasometer, tea machinery and fan-making works, aerated waters factory, dry dock, handkerchief

factory and shipyard (launching vessels which were the largest man-made moving objects on earth).[48]

Ulster – and Belfast in particular – had a lot to lose if Home Rule upset this astonishing boom. Tellingly, the Ulster Covenant of 1912 began with the words 'Being convinced in our consciences that Home Rule would be disastrous to the material well-being of Ulster'. Religious fears were significant and genuine. But from the outset, this question was inseparably bound up with economic prosperity.

While Northern Ireland's founding fathers might be proud that what they built has endured for more than a century, they would surely weep at how the economic dynamism of the six counties has collapsed. Northern Ireland's GDP – the total wealth it produces each year – is about £56 billion: lower than that of Lithuania.[49] The Republic's GDP is ten times that of Northern Ireland, even though its population is just over two and a half times bigger.[50]

Unionists, and some sceptical economists, will question whether the gulf is quite so big because much of this involves what seems artificial – the movement in and out of the Republic of money sent to the island to avoid higher tax rates elsewhere. It's true that this means such capital is more mobile than something like a factory (although there are plenty of those too). But the unavoidable reality is that this hard cash is benefiting the Irish exchequer, and is being used to build up public services. Even if it were to stop tomorrow this money would have already bequeathed a vast legacy of tangible benefits in roads, schools, hospitals and the like.

The roots of Northern Ireland's economic decline lie far further back than the Troubles. A moribund government that knew it was guaranteed perpetual power focused on petty sectarianism while presiding over industrial decline. Right from the outset, the basics of good government weren't quite what they seemed. One of the most distinguished civil servants from Northern Ireland's first half-century, John Oliver, recalled that from the

The case for a united Ireland

beginning Northern Ireland's financial relationship with London was 'shrouded in secrecy and protected by a veil of nothing less than make-believe'.[51] The Royal Commission on the British Constitution in the early 1970s found 'the collapse of the financial arrangements laid down' and 'the maintenance of a facade'.[52]

By contrast, the Republic has demonstrated how self-determination is in itself an economic advantage, allowing fiscal agility that spots gaps and exploits them. The South has shown itself to be an environment fundamentally more conducive to prosperity than the North. This is about a mindset that goes beyond corporation tax.

People in Newry are as clever as people in Dundalk; people in Dungannon are as entrepreneurial as people in Athlone; people in Ballymena are as hard-working as people in Cork. The reason for the economic disparity on the island can only be systemic, with the talents of the Northern population held back by a broken system.

Since 1938, Britain has subsidised Northern Ireland's existence with ever-increasing largesse.[53] That many unionists now cling to this as an argument against unity speaks to an ineffable lack of ambition.

Some of the more venal unionist political figures have been caught boasting about milking the Treasury for what they can get. Such economic dependence is stultifying. As it spends other people's money, Stormont has become haughtily profligate. It has produced poor results through populist polices – but then blamed the Treasury in London for not sending even more cash for it to waste.

The public inquiry into the 'cash for ash' scandal led to the humiliating exposure of endemic incompetence in Stormont's political and bureaucratic classes alike. It was a moment that should have prompted radical change; instead, the system has largely carried on in the manner to which it has become accustomed. Stormont has become a habitation of hopelessness, yet without it there seems no way in which Northern Ireland can be governed with the consent of the majority of its inhabitants.

Disruption is transitory

Al Smith, the legendary early-twentieth-century governor of New York, once described childbirth as a mother 'going down into the valley of death that a new pair of eyes might look out upon the world'.[54] The birth of a new country entails some of the same inevitable trauma. But, as with a new child, this new country would be imbued with potential.

Only the most obtusely unimaginative would deny that starting anew has the potential to create something far better than what now exists. There would unquestionably be a major cost to unifying the island. But what was once a fiscal impossibility is now financially achievable, even if it could involve short-term pain.

Northern Ireland's £14 billion annual subsidy from London is a substantial sum. There is academic dispute as to how much of that could be whittled away by negotiation or because certain of its costs – such as expenditure on the Royal Family or nuclear weapons – simply wouldn't exist in a united Ireland. But even if that was the total figure, it would be paid for by a Republic whose GDP now stands at more than €550 billion.

Never in its history has Ireland been wealthier. Even Esmond Birnie, a former Ulster Unionist Assemblyman who is now Ulster University's chief economist, accepts that 'In economic terms the argument for the Union remains but the real strength of that argument has declined.'[55]

The acceptance by the EU in 2017 that if there is a united Ireland then Northern Ireland will automatically rejoin the EU binds that powerful bloc to make the transition as smooth as possible. The EU will have a stake in this new country, which will provide an important opportunity for Brussels to demonstrate that it can integrate Northern Ireland in peace and prosperity.

There would be massive global goodwill, creating across Europe and beyond a sense of excitement akin to that which accompanied German reunification. For the US, financial support for unity won't just be about misty-eyed memories of the old land. American administrations tend to be hard-headed about their self-interest;

The case for a united Ireland

they will know that if they don't contribute to the fledgling new country and it is suitably desperate then it will turn elsewhere for that support. The last thing the US wants is an enhanced role for a rival like China.

Likewise, as many as one in four British people are of Irish descent. Hundreds of thousands of those now living in Britain were born in Ireland.[56] These are people no longer just building the roads and tunnels, but sitting in boardrooms and in government. There will be goodwill from significant individuals and institutions of influence.

John Hume once described the Irish as 'the biggest wandering people in the world – we're a much bigger wandering people than the Jews'.[57] That brings remarkable opportunities. Just as Israel has a global network of sympathetic supporters, so Ireland would have a substantial diaspora in every part of the globe. There would be scope to raise money for the unity transition through unity bonds, which would allow Ireland to borrow at competitive rates while allowing the diaspora, businesses and foreign nations to not only support the process of unification but make a relatively safe financial investment, given Ireland's global economic credibility.

Post-unity, there are good reasons to believe that Ireland and Britain would retain strong relations. Not only are there compelling geographic reasons to do so, but the two states would retain shared commitments under the Good Friday Agreement.

The US fought the British to surrender in the eighteenth century, yet still holds a uniquely close bond with Britain. Relationships forged over centuries are difficult to fully sunder even in war. Britain and Ireland's ties of kinship and trade and language and manners and outlook and myriad other facts of our existence survived the War of Independence and the Troubles: they're very likely to survive a peaceful and democratic transfer of sovereignty over what is now less than 3% of the UK.

Sam McBride

Endless possibility

The comedian Tim McGarry once quipped that the definition of success in Northern Ireland is 'passed off peacefully'. It's funny because it's true. But what's not funny is the poverty of ambition betrayed by such a defensive mindset. When success is measured by the absence of violence, then no matter how paltry the substance of what exists, it will be deemed acceptable. For a growing number of people, many of whom were not even born when the Troubles were raging, such narrow vision is no longer enough. They want more, and they've every right to want more.

Creating a new country isn't something to be done flippantly. It cannot be compared to dislike for a passing government or for one's neighbours. It's not even to be done because the neighbouring jurisdiction can offer some short-term bounty. There must be compelling and enduring reasons to embrace the toil necessary for such an endeavour.

This is a decision that has involved centuries of consideration, but, at previous points in our history, securing an independent and united Ireland either was impossible or would have been dangerously irresponsible to pursue. Now it is demonstrably possible, and the mechanisms exist not only to secure that outcome, but to incentivise those doing so to achieve unity by persuasion and compromise rather than at the end of a pike or a gun barrel.

If a referendum date is given, the urgency of the question will focus intense thinking on what should happen and the possibilities it will bring. There is inbuilt inertia in public life. The Covid-19 pandemic demonstrated how in certain circumstances transformative societal and economic changes can be achieved within weeks.

For Northern Ireland, unity would mean immediately rejoining the EU. That's not just about increased wealth, but about the sort of expansive and open-minded country we want to be part of. It's about a union big enough to take on Big Tech and global monopolies. And it's about the clout to set and enforce robust environmental protections.

In a century that will be defined by climate change, Ireland's environmental record is lamentable. In Northern Ireland, Lough Neagh has been turned into a luminescent green toilet of toxicity, an emblem of how cack-handed Stormont policies have trashed a beautiful landscape.

As the ecological economist Seán Fearon has argued, even if Northern Ireland's regional administration suddenly had the will to take drastic action on climate change and environmental degradation, it would never be able to secure the financial capital necessary to undertake work at the scale required. A sovereign state would be very different.[58]

Yet the Republic has wallowed in mercantile hedonism at the expense of its famously green land. An economy centred on ever-increasing levels of consumption is pushed by those who pretend to care about the environment, despite the inherent contradiction. As multinationals wield more and more power, 21% of all electricity – more than that of every urban home combined – is going to data centres. Despite Ireland's vast wealth, it is still choosing to burn coal – the filthiest way to produce electricity. Even having the Green Party in coalition has done little to deliver the radical measures necessary to redress such fundamental society-wide flaws.

The creation of a new country would mean an unprecedented opportunity to start from first principles and ask what sort of Ireland do we want for our children and our grandchildren – one that is laden with gold but ecologically dead, or a land in which there might not be such extreme wealth, but that is sustainable and prepared for the looming climatic challenges?

A future abounding in possibility

A year before his death in 1918, John Redmond, the great nationalist leader whose life's work was securing Home Rule, reflected: 'The life of a politician, especially of an Irish politician, is one long series of postponements and compromises and disappointments and disillusions. As we grow old, and this of course bears in upon me, we feel our ideals grow dimmer and more blurred, and perhaps many of them disappearing one by one.'[59] There is a pathos in that sentiment that was amplified by his despair at how decades of diligent labour had been snatched away, first by world war and then by the Easter Rising.

For centuries, there was an Irish ethos of noble but ultimately pointless struggle towards a goal that was likely unattainable. In recent decades, the island has broken those shackles. Ireland can regularly defeat England at rugby, and even occasionally at cricket. Where it matters far more – in negotiating the post-Brexit trading landscape – Irish officials and ministers comprehensively outclassed their UK counterparts.

Economically, Ireland is forging far ahead of the UK. The old expectation of failure is alien to today's Ireland, even if there is a rich appreciation of how blessed we are in this age after centuries in which our ancestors struggled to keep breath in their bodies.

Having for centuries sent its sons and daughters abroad, Ireland is now a beacon and a refuge; for example, the Republic took in almost six times as many Ukrainian refugees per head of population as the UK.[60]

There is much to unite this island. Some fifteen centuries after his death, its patron saint provides a template for how former foes can not just live in peace, but grow to love one another. Despite having been seized from his home in Britain and enslaved by Irish raiders, Patrick came to have compassion for those who had mistreated him – and they grew to respect him. In one of his two surviving writings, Patrick spoke of his 'love of my neighbours who are my only sons — for them I gave up my home country, my parents and even pushing [*sic*] my own life to the brink of death'.[61] Even in post-Christian Ireland, there's hardly a more apt example of how enmity can be healed by a decision to turn the other cheek.

Patrick's life also rebukes the sectarianism of those who tell the British to go home, or who shout 'Up the 'RA' in the faces of IRA victims. If the Brits had been sent packing 1,500 years ago, Patrick would have been among their number. Our history across these islands is far more intertwined than the propagandists can ever admit.

Patrick's story should lead to a renewed understanding of how the Irish are themselves in many cases a migrant people – from England, Scotland, France, Scandinavia and more distant lands. Those coming today from Africa, Eastern Europe or Asia are following millennia of others who came to this isle in search of a better life.

If it comes, Irish unity will not be an end to history. It will not solve all the island's ills or erase the hatred some of its inhabitants have for their neighbours. The unity now possible is not that of the zealot. It is not a unity of Pearse or de Valera or Gerry Adams. In many ways, it is a rejection of the Ireland they envisaged. When King George V came to Belfast in 1921, he desired 'that my coming to Ireland to-day may prove to be the first step towards the end of strife amongst her people, whatever their race or creed'. The king, who had involved himself personally in the resolution of the Irish crisis, went on: 'In that hope I appeal to all Irishmen to pause, to stretch out the hand of forbearance and conciliation, to forgive and forget, and to join in making for the land they love a new era of peace, contentment and goodwill.'[62]

That, as we know, wasn't what happened. But it provides the basis on which a new country could be founded. Ancient feuds must someday be resolved: if not by us, then by our children or their children – who might look back and wonder at our lethargy.

3.
The case for a united Ireland

FINTAN O'TOOLE

'It is true that we are part of one island, it is true that we are all Irish.' This statement from 1956 was obviously made by an Irish nationalist – except that, in this case, the obvious is deceptive. The writer was Brian Maginess, the solidly unionist minister for finance of Northern Ireland, and the words are in an official publication of the Stormont government called *Why the border must be: the Northern Ireland case in brief*. It was issued to counter attempts by the coalition government in Dublin to create sympathy for Irish unity in Britain. Maginess' essay was included with the text of a statement by the prime minister of Northern Ireland, Viscount Brookeborough.

What is striking about this argument from the heart of unionism is that neither Brookeborough nor Maginess contested the idea that it was logical to think of the island of Ireland as a single country. Brookeborough quoted with approval the words of a fellow unionist, his minister for home affairs, Walter Topping:

> In circumstances other than those that exist in Ireland it would be natural to assume that an island the size of this one should be economically and politically a single entity. Much can be said for the practical advantages to be gained by the elimination of the Border; and there is also the sentimental appeal of being Irish throughout (a sentiment which the Scotsman and the Welshman proudly maintain) had the situation been different – had being Irish not been made incompatible with being at the same time British.

This, of course, raises a question that is now much more salient: what if being Irish can be made compatible with being British? What if the divide between competing mentalities and identities has become bridgeable?

Partition, Brookeborough insisted in 1956, was necessary because there were, on either side of the border, fundamentally different ways of thinking: 'The border between Northern Ireland and Eire exists because of the ideological gulf which divides the two peoples.' Maginess in his contribution to the same pamphlet was even more explicit: 'Partition is based not upon geographical, racial or language differences, but on differences of ideas.'

For him, this difference concerned not just what people thought but their ability to think freely at all:

> We have no press censorship in Northern Ireland. People can write what they like, subject to keeping within the common law. We may or may not agree with what we read, but we have the opportunity of reading it. That opportunity does not exist in Eire, where your reading is chosen for you ... The right to knowledge, this right of mental liberty, is regarded as fundamental in the North. In the South it is subject to so many qualifications that it has ceased to be a right at all. [These] differences ... show a complete separation of thought and ideas, and such precludes any possibility of union.[1]

Maginess was largely right. The Republic of Ireland (as it had recently become) did indeed have fierce official censorship of books and magazines. Many important works by contemporary Irish novelists and short story writers were banned in their own country. And this censorship was part of a larger nexus of limits on the freedom of citizens that included the banning of contraceptives and the constitutional prohibition on divorce. 'The right of mental liberty' may have been rather less 'fundamental in the North' than Maginess claimed, but it was easy to look south and see an obscurantist Catholic state that did not seem quite to belong to the post-war liberal order of the democratic world.

It is, nonetheless, highly significant that even at the height of its own prestige in the aftermath of Northern Ireland's part in the Allied victory in the Second World War, the case for partition rested, essentially, on what was inside people's heads: the 'ideological gulf', the 'differences of ideas'. These terms were, of course, codes for a religious divide that was, and remains, real. But they implicitly conceded that Irish unity would make sense if it were not for distinctions of mentality that made it impossible. And this concession raises a basic question for the twenty-first century: if partition is all in the mind, what sense does it make when the Irish have changed their minds so radically?

One apparently good answer would be to point to the undoubted truth that these 'differences of ideas' were underpinned by potent actualities. Northern Ireland was a product of the fusion of three forces: demographic, economic and political. It was made possible by the existence of a secure Protestant majority in the north-east of the island; the radical superiority of the Northern economy over its Southern counterpart; and the firm alliance between Ulster unionism and British conservatism. But the stark reality is that each of these three pillars has now crumbled.

Who are the people now?

In that 1956 pamphlet, Brookeborough invoked the idea of the inhabitants of Northern Ireland as a distinctive people: 'the union with Great Britain is preserved not by a British garrison but by the declared will of the Northern Ireland people, expressed through their elected Parliament – and that will is paramount'.[2] In one sense, if he were alive today, he could claim vindication. The idea that it is the people of Northern Ireland whose votes will determine whether or not the Union continues is now common cause. It is accepted by the Irish and British governments and by the vast majority of Irish nationalists. But in another sense, Brookeborough would surely be shocked to discover who those people now are.

Before the late nineteenth century, no one seriously thought of the inhabitants of the six north-eastern counties of Ireland as a sovereign people. Even the Ulster Covenant signed in 1912 and described by the historian Alvin Jackson as the 'birth certificate' of Northern Ireland refers in its opening words to two spatial categories that in fact differ from what became the six counties: 'Being convinced in our consciences that Home Rule would be disastrous

Religious affiliation in the six counties that now constitute Northern Ireland, 1861–2021

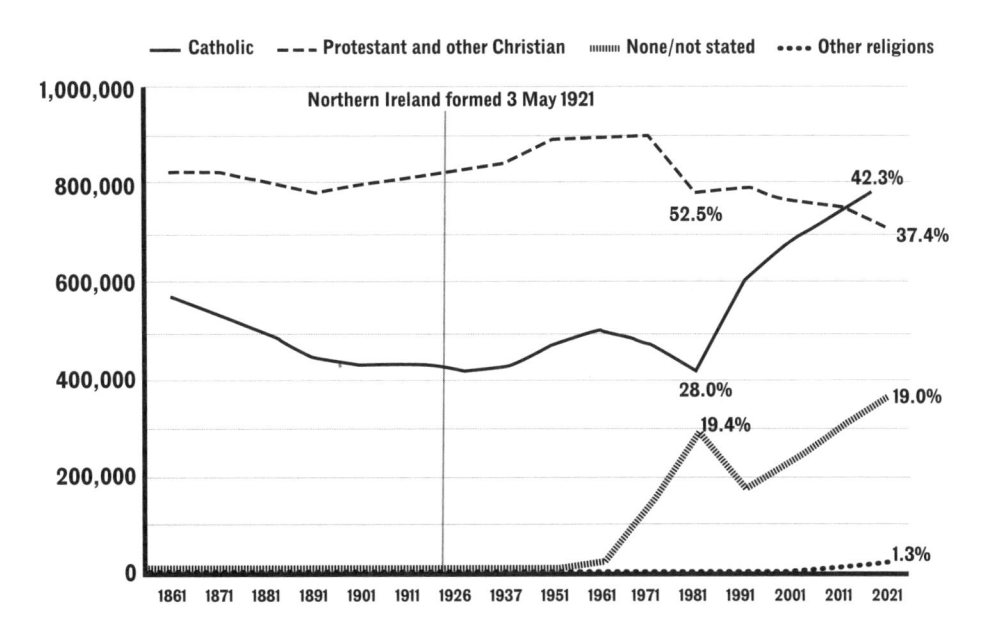

Legend: —— Catholic --- Protestant and other Christian ||||| None/not stated •••• Other religions

Northern Ireland formed 3 May 1921

Protestant and other Christian: 52.5% (c. 1981), 37.4% (2021)
Catholic: 28.0% (c. 1981), 42.3% (2021)
None/not stated: 19.4% (c. 1981), 19.0% (2021)
Other religions: 1.3% (2021)

Note: The kinks in the graph at 1971 and 1981 are explained by the refusal of some members of the Catholic community to participate in the Census. This was particularly marked in 1981, the time of the hunger strikes. It led to a marked under-counting of Catholics and, as a consequence, an over-counting of those with no religion. Source: NISRA.

to the material well-being of Ulster as well as of the whole of Ireland'.[3] Ulster is not coterminous with what became Northern Ireland and the evocation of 'the whole of Ireland' implies the recognition of the island as a political entity.

The creation of Northern Ireland was less a case of a people forging a state than of a statelet forging a people. This was true in two ways. First, opposition to Home Rule brought historically antagonistic Presbyterians and Anglicans together into a single overarching Protestant cause. Second, Northern Ireland was then imagined not as either a historic or a geographic unit but simply as the largest continuous area that could be guaranteed to contain a secure Protestant and unionist majority for the foreseeable future.

But Northern Ireland's unforeseeable future has arrived. The 1926 Census, the first after partition, showed that Catholics, totalling 420,428 people, constituted 33.5% of the population of Northern Ireland. By 2021, Catholics, totalling 805,151, constituted 42.3% of the population. When religion and 'upbringing' are combined, 45.7% of the population are 'Catholic', compared with 43.5% who are 'Protestant, Other Christian or Christian-related'. Almost one in five people in Northern Ireland either has no religion or declines to state a religious affiliation.

What this means is that the 'Northern Ireland people' as Brookeborough understood the term in the 1950s – the solid, permanent Protestant majority called into being by partition – no longer exists. And it is unlikely ever to be reconstituted. Each of the three major Protestant denominations – Church of Ireland, Presbyterian and Methodist – is in slow but steady decline. Even in the 20 years between the Censuses of 2001 and 2021, the proportion of Protestants (defined by both practice and upbringing) in Northern Ireland declined by almost 10 percentage points, from 53.0% to 43.5%.[4]

It does not follow that a united Ireland is inevitable or that the continuing Protestant and British identity of so many people in Northern Ireland can be dismissed as an anachronism. But it is obvious that the demographic ground has shifted irrevocably.

What happened to economic superiority?

When Ireland was partitioned, the north-east of Ireland was an industrial powerhouse and, to put it very mildly, the rest of the island was not. This economic gulf made the two parts of Ireland genuinely very different. And it underpinned the arguments for partition. Intertwined with religious and ideological divisions, there were solid reasons to believe that an urbanised region with a modern economy, serving British imperial markets, could not sit easily in an independent or autonomous Ireland in which agriculture and food production held primacy.

The case for a united Ireland

The greatest passenger ships yet built, RMS *Olympic* and RMS *Titanic*, were launched in Belfast in May 1911 and April 1912, respectively. The York Street linen mill, which employed 4,000 workers, was the biggest of its kind anywhere in the world, while William Ewart's mill on the Crumlin Road was almost as large. During the First World War, Ulster's linen industry employed an astonishing 90,000 workers.

In Belfast, 70% of female workers and 36% of male workers were employed in manufacturing. The comparable figures for Dublin were 32% and 20%. Belfast, which was then larger than Dublin, had global-scale shipbuilding, ropeworks, engineering, textile and mineral water industries. In the South, the first census of industrial production in the Irish Free State revealed that brewing (in effect Guinness) accounted for almost 30% of all output. In 1924, live animals and manufactured, processed or simply prepared food and drink accounted for six-sevenths of exports from the Free State.

In the early years of Irish independence, attempts to industrialise were stymied by the onset of the Great Depression. The biggest manufacturing concern attracted into the Free State, the Cork-based Irish subsidiary of Henry Ford & Sons, looked like a harbinger of glorious success in 1930 when it was producing about 3,000 tractors a month and employing nearly 7,000 men. But most were laid off as the Great Depression took hold, and by 1931 Ford provided intermittent employment for only 1,250 workers.[5] The sterotypes of the North as modern and the South as backward were crude, yet they were not too far out of kilter with the broad nature of the two economies.

But over the past half-century, two fundamental shifts have happened. First, Northern Ireland lost much of its industrial base. Manufacturing employment fell from 169,000 in 1970, to 101,000 in 2000 and to 89,000 in 2024. There are thus fewer workers in all sectors of Northern Ireland's manufacturing industry now than were employed in linen-making alone during the First World War. The shrinkage of the linen and shipbuilding sectors as providers of jobs is reflected in the drop in employment in textiles and clothing from 58,300 in 1970 to 3,600 in 2019, and in 'transport equipment' other than motor vehicles from 14,300 to 7,400. Overall, the share of manufacturing in total employment in Northern Ireland dropped from 35% in 1970 to 16% in 2000 and 11% in 2022. The North is no longer an industrial society.

And the South is no longer an agricultural society. Agriculture still employed a quarter of the workforce when the Republic joined the European Communities in 1973. The subsequent decline has been dramatic: agriculture accounted for just 4% of the workforce in 2022, slightly below the overall level for the EU as a whole. Food processing remains important – the agrifood sector accounts for 6.5% of employment in the Republic and about the same proportion of gross national income. But ironically, if we judge it by export figures, Northern Ireland is now more dependent on agriculture than the Republic is: food and beverages account for 23% of the North's exports, compared with 8% of the South's.[6]

Conversely, the South is now more industrial than the North. By far the biggest part of its economy is in services, but industry nonetheless accounts for 19% of the workforce, compared with 11% in the North.

This shift is not just in the kinds of jobs people do. It is also about where and how they live. In 1966, the South was still a rural society, with less than half the population living in towns or cities. By 2016, two-thirds of the population was urban. As it happens, this is almost exactly the same as in the North. In everything that comes with urban life – from patterns of employment to ideas of community and belonging, to types of housing, to the nitty-gritty of the daily grind – the once yawning gaps between North and South have shrunk to nothing.

The bond between unionism and conservatism is broken

Traditionally, the Conservative and Unionist Party (to give it its full title) held to the line succinctly summed up by Margaret Thatcher in 1981: 'Northern Ireland is part of the United Kingdom – as much as my constituency is.'[7] This was never really true but, by 1990, the Conservatives were officially articulating a position in which Northern Ireland was very different from Thatcher's English constituency of Finchley. It was (and is) inconceivable that any British government would state that Finchley was free to go its own way and join, for example, France. In 1990, however, the then secretary of state for Northern Ireland, Peter Brooke, announced, in a carefully crafted phrase, that 'The British government has no selfish strategic or economic interest in Northern Ireland.'[8] This position ultimately became one of the building blocks of the Belfast Agreement of 1998.

But the underlying implication was not spelled out: Northern Ireland had a semi-detached place within the Union. Its position was contingent, qualified and impermanent. And this is what became explicit in the crisis over Brexit after the referendum of 2016. Two successive British prime ministers, Theresa May and Boris Johnson, insisted that no one in their position could ever agree to Northern Ireland remaining with the EU's single market and customs union while Britain departed from them. Yet that is, in effect, what happened. The Northern Ireland Protocol and the creation of the so-called 'border in the Irish Sea' mean that, when it comes to the regulation of trade and relations with the EU, Northern Ireland is now more closely aligned with the Republic than it is with Britain. And this is a dynamic process – as EU laws change and Northern Ireland adapts to them, the differences between it and the rest of the UK will widen over time.

What should be noted about the process that led to this extraordinary development is how cold-blooded it was. The Protocol was highly controversial in Northern Ireland – but not so in Britain. The conservative political nexus in England protested its love for the Union, but in the end did not protest too much. Given a choice between 'getting Brexit done' and strengthening Britain's ties to Northern Ireland, it ritually wrung its hands before using them to grasp the prize of Brexit. In the context of a united Ireland, what this recent history has shown is that unionism in Northern

Ireland cannot rely on its traditional allies in Britain. Its belief in an indissoluble bond is not shared on the far side of the Irish Sea.

At one level, Brexit was a brutal reminder that, contrary to Brookeborough's claim that 'the Northern Ireland people' determined their own political status, it is a subordinate part of the UK. Northern Ireland voted by a clear majority to remain in the EU but was nonetheless taken out of it against its collective will. Yet for many unionists – especially those who support the DUP – the bluntness of this demonstration of the limits of Northern Ireland's freedom to determine its own destiny was more than compensated for by the hope of a double exit. Brexit would not simply mean the UK's departure from the EU. It would also be an act of separation from the Republic. It would reverse the slow drift towards integration on the island. The Republic would stay on the European train while Northern Ireland would hitch its wagon to the renewed and reinvented Global Britain. In this fantasy, partition would be rekindled and reinvigorated: with the border no longer a mere line between the island's two polities but a stout frontier between the EU and the UK.

Yet this gamble now looks much more like the last throw of the dice for a unionism reliant on the good faith and affection of English conservatism. Brexit revealed how, in a British political crisis, Northern Ireland unionism really didn't matter very much. We know from the survey evidence that English people who voted Leave in 2016 or supported the Tories in the 2017 general election did not feel any great sense of obligation to the Union with Northern Ireland.

The most telling measure of commitment to a political union is whether you are content for taxes from its richest part to be used to subsidise services in the poorest. In the 2018 Future of England study, just 25% of Leave voters, and 29% of people who said they voted Conservative in 2017, agreed with the proposition: 'Revenue raised from taxpayers in England should also be distributed to Northern Ireland to help Northern Irish public services.' And, rather startlingly, when asked whether 'the unravelling of the peace process in Northern Ireland' is a 'price worth paying' for a

Brexit that allows them to 'take back control', fully 83% of Leave voters and 73% of Conservative voters agreed that it was.[9]

In a Channel 4/Survation study of November 2018, voters were asked how concerned they would be 'If Brexit leads to Northern Ireland leaving the United Kingdom and joining the Republic of Ireland'. Just a third of Leave voters said they would be very concerned or quite concerned. Fully 61% said they would be not very concerned or not at all concerned. Of the four grades of concern offered by the pollsters, by far the most popular among Leave voters, with 36%, was 'not at all concerned'.[10] And in a YouGov survey of Conservative Party members in June 2019, a startling 59% said that 'Northern Ireland leaving the United Kingdom' was a price they were willing to pay for Brexit.[11]

There may still lurk within English conservatism a sentimental and rhetorical attachment to Northern Ireland's place within the Union – but when political expedience dictates otherwise, sentiments and rhetoric prove to be of little consequence. Ulster unionism has to look for a very different way to secure its long-term interests and, indeed, its place in a profoundly changed world. That requires a recognition that political identities on the island of Ireland have also changed. This in turn brings us back to the issue that seemed so favourable to unionism in the 1950s – the belief that there is a fundamental difference of mentalities and attitudes between North and South.

What does Irish identity mean now?

James Connolly, writing in 1914, argued that partition 'would mean a carnival of reaction both North and South, would set back the wheels of progress, would ... paralyse all advanced movements whilst it endured'.[12] It would be hard to argue that Connolly was wrong. Even if the deep religious and economic divisions made it inevitable, partition allowed both North and South to cohere around opposite poles of a binary choice: Protestant/unionist or Catholic/nationalist. Neither of the new polities had to develop a pluralist idea of citizenship, equally open to those of all religious and ethical traditions.

But those binaries have lost their grip. In the North, since 2006, 'neither unionist nor nationalist' has been the identity expressed by the largest number of respondents to the annual Northern Ireland Life and Times (NILT) surveys. The number choosing this identity (or non-identity) peaked at 50% during the Brexit crisis in 2018 – in 2023 it stood at 37%, still comfortably ahead of unionist (30%) and nationalist (28%).[13]

Likewise, the British/Irish binary has been greatly complicated by the rise of a specific Northern Irish identity. The 2021 Census showed a marked rise in the number of people expressing a complex sense of national identity: 'British and Northern Irish' or 'Irish and Northern Irish' or 'British, Irish and Northern Irish'.[14] This is borne out in the ARINS/*The Irish Times* survey of 2023, which showed that if the full range of positive responses is taken into account, a slight majority (52%) identify strongly or fairly strongly as Northern Irish, whereas 48% identify as Irish and 46% as British.[15] Significantly, this Northern Irish identity is attractive to both sides of the traditional divide: two-fifths of Catholics and two-thirds of Protestants rated it highly.

In the South, unsurprisingly, the overwhelming identity as revealed in the ARINS/*The Irish Times* survey is simply 'Irish'. (On a 1–10 scale, 78% give it a 10 and 93% pick 6 or higher.) But this Irishness has detached itself from what was for so long its inseparable twin. It is not 'Irish Catholic'. The proportion of the population that identifies itself as Catholic has dropped from well over 90% in the Census of 1991 to below 70% in 2022.[16] But even these figures understate the scale of change. Weekly Mass attendance by Catholics is now down to somewhere between 30 and 40%. No priest was ordained in the Dublin archdiocese in 2024 and only two had been ordained since 2020.[17] Most importantly, Catholicism is no longer a mainstream *political* identity in the Republic. The decisive votes in the referendums in 2015 to permit same-sex marriage and in 2018 to overturn the constitutional ban on abortion (both carried by two-thirds majorities) marked the end of the fusion of religion and politics in Irish national identity.

Those votes also reflected a deeper reality: political struggles on both parts of the island have never been only about competing national identities. Gender and sexuality have always been arenas for the contestation of power. In Connolly's 'carnival of reaction', both Northern Ireland and the Republic were highly patriarchal and male-dominated societies – even more so than was the case in Britain. Homosexual acts were decriminalised in England and Wales in 1967 – but not until 1982 in Northern Ireland and not until 1993 in the Republic. Legal discrimination against women was generally worse in the South than in the North, but many of the same inequalities were entrenched on both sides of the border. The Irish Women's Liberation Movement and the Northern Ireland Women's Movement fought the same battles against patriarchal control of reproduction, domestic violence, poor childcare and inequalities in employment and the workplace.

These histories of common struggles bear on the possibilities of a united Ireland because they have gradually altered the nature of public life on both sides of the border. It is still male-dominated and there is a long way to go before full equality is achieved. But a third of the members of the Northern Ireland Assembly are female, as are the first and deputy first ministers. The Republic has yet to have a female taoiseach (though it has had two female presidents since 1990) and only 25% of the TDs elected to the Dáil in 2024 are women. (Fourteen constituencies have no women TDs at all.) Nonetheless, however slow and incomplete the process, the long-term trend is moving away from the stultifyingly patriarchal politics that did so much to prop up the binary identities that sustained partition.

Ireland is now, moreover, a multicultural society. The old monolith in which well over 90% of the population was Catholic and white has crumbled. Twenty per cent of those who live in Ireland were born elsewhere – amounting to over a million people. There are more people of foreign birth living in the Republic than there are Catholics in Northern Ireland. Nearly a quarter of the population has an ethnicity other than white Irish. Three-quarters of a million people speak a language other than English or Irish at home.

When the Constitution was changed in 1998 to embrace the aspiration for the island to be shared by all those who inhabit it in 'all the diversity of their identities and traditions', the framers of this phrase may not have anticipated just how diverse those people would become and how many traditions – religious, cultural, national, historical – they might embody. Between the North and South poles of opposing Protestant and Catholic collective selves there is a whole world of complex, fluid and hyphenated identities.

There is another element in this mix: the idea of a European belonging. Admittedly it can be seen not as a binding force between North and South but as itself a source of division. Commenting on the ARINS/*The Irish Times* survey of 2023, John Garry, Brendan O'Leary and Jamie Pow noted that

> extremely few Northern Protestants very strongly identify as European (only 4%). The proportion rises to just 12% once the whole positive spectrum of the scale (6–10) is taken into account. Two-thirds of Protestants are 'not at all' European. In contrast, many Southerners feel European: one-quarter 'very strongly' so, and two-thirds fairly or very strongly (6–10), while two-fifths of Northern Catholics are fairly or very strongly European. It is therefore currently implausible to see the European identity as playing a strong bridging role under possible Irish unification.[18]

And yet, as Katy Hayward and Ben Rosher note in their analysis of the 2023 NILT survey, 'one aspect of political identity that has changed the most dramatically over the past 25 years has been that of Europeanness'. In 2002, only 7% of respondents said they always thought of themselves as European compared with two-thirds (67%) who never did. But in 2023, almost a third (31%) always thought of themselves in that way, compared with 37% who never did.[19]

This survey does not really contradict the ARINS/*The Irish Times* findings, which also showed sharp differences in the 'Europeanness' of unionists and nationalists. But the NILT survey does show some significant things. One is that there is a vastly increased sense of a European identity in the North – at the very least, it is an extra layer of complication in the way many people think about their sense of belonging. Another is that this sense of being European is strongly felt among those who refuse to define themselves as either unionist or nationalist – the group that will surely make up the decisive swing voter bloc in any border poll. Over half (52%) of the 'Neithers' said that they always or sometimes think of themselves as European. In a context where Donald Trump's second presidency has been marked by a sharp rise in America's antagonism towards its traditional European allies – and a consequent realisation that Britain has to move back towards closer alignment with Europe – it seems likely that this dimension of identity will become even more important.

One of the many ironies of Brexit is that it led to a rapid increase in the willingness of people in the North to hold Irish passports. The number holding an Irish passport, either solely or jointly with a British passport, jumped from 375,800 in 2011 to 614,300 in 2021.[20] Much of this increase can be understood as a pragmatic response to Brexit – it is more convenient for travellers to the continent to hold EU passports. But pragmatism is itself highly meaningful. It points to an underlying flexibility about national affiliation. People make choices about identity based on history and culture – but also on the real circumstances of their lives.

If we stand back from all of this, what we see is that there are many movies playing in the Irish multiplex. The old classics of Protestant/unionist and Catholic/nationalist are still on show. But the other screens are projecting more complex pictures of Northern Irishness, Southern pluralism, Europeanness, migrant hyphenated identities and good old-fashioned hard-headed pragmatism. The future does not look either green or orange but more like the development of a rainbow nation.

Fintan O'Toole

Would Britishness survive?

We know that Britishness – in the sense of a vibrant connection to the cultures of Scotland, England and Wales – can survive a departure from the UK because it already has. The 26 counties left the UK in 1922 but they did not cease to be closely engaged with the neighbouring island physically (in the form of emigration), economically, but also culturally. The Irish language (in spite of the efforts of successive Irish governments) did not become the dominant vernacular. English continued to reign, and now that it is effectively the global lingua franca there is no doubt that it would retain its primacy in a united Ireland.

Clamour for the BBC and ITV was so strong in the South that the state set up a TV channel (RTÉ 2) to rebroadcast many of their programmes. (Those who could also set up large aerials on their houses to pirate British TV programmes.) British newspapers still circulate widely in Ireland – some of them even have special Irish editions. British trade unions still organise many workplaces and professions in the Republic. Irish fans still support English and Scottish football teams and Irish youngsters still aspire to play for them. Irish writers still send their books to London publishers and Irish readers still buy books by British authors. And, secretly or otherwise, many Irish people are as obsessed as the most fervent loyalist in the North with the Royal Family.

And, of course, British popular culture is also very Irish. English comedy, from Oliver Goldsmith, Richard Brinsley Sheridan and Oscar Wilde to Spike Milligan, Steve Coogan and Caroline Aherne, has a deeply Irish streak. The same is true of English popular music, from Dusty Springfield and The Beatles to John Lydon and Oasis. The BBC would hardly be the same without Terry Wogan, Graham Norton and many other Irish presenters, or without Irish journalists like Fergal Keane, Orla Guerin and Caitriona Perry.

This is all very obvious: perhaps so obvious that it is seldom even mentioned in the context of Irish unity. But it bears emphasis. In the Irish context, 'Britishness' is not just that set of symbols that has to be delicately managed in the process of unification. It's much more robust than that. Sheer proximity, linguistic similarity, historic and institutional connection, the intimacy of family ties across the Irish Sea and the simple fact that Britain is a bigger market that will always act as a lure for Irish talent mean that there is absolutely no danger that these ties will be weakened, let alone cut. People in Northern Ireland who think of themselves as British will no more lose that connection after unification than people in the rest of Ireland did after 1922.

What do Southerners really want?

We know from the survey evidence that support for a united Ireland in the Republic is both very broad and very shallow. On the one hand, polling (including the ARINS/*The Irish Times* surveys) consistently shows that around two-thirds of respondents say they would vote for it in a referendum. On the other, when 'terms and conditions apply', these same prospective voters tend to take fright. The possibility of tax rises puts them off. But so does even the idea of altering the symbols of nationality such as the national anthem, the Irish tricolour or membership for the unified state in the Commonwealth (see Chapter 1). And the idea that a subsidiary devolved administration might continue for the six counties does not appeal either. It seems that Southern voters like the deal until they begin to read the small print.

We will come to the big issue of taxation and the financing of the process of unification shortly. But let's think about these questions of symbolism and of political and institutional structures. How big an obstacle is Southern resistance to change really likely to pose?

We might answer this question with another: how much have most Southern voters actually thought about the process of unification? As we saw in Chapter 1, not much. 'The findings of the 2021 deliberative forum, published as part of the ARINS project, show that of the 46 people who participated, 28 indicated before the deliberations that they were either not at all or not very well informed' about the issues. 'Generally, the participants were surprised to learn that there are different possible versions of a united Ireland.'[21]

This lack of engagement may be regarded by enthusiasts on different sides of the argument as reprehensible, but it is hardly mysterious. In the exit poll conducted for the Irish general election in November 2024, voters listed their top ten political priorities as housing and homelessness, the cost of living, healthcare, economic stability, immigration, climate change, crime, local transport, childcare, and value for money in public spending.[22] A united Ireland did not feature. It is not what the vast majority of Southerners are thinking about when they think about politics.

The ARINS/*The Irish Times* surveys specifically offer 'achieving a united Ireland' and 'preparing for a united Ireland' among nine possible priorities, with respondents invited to choose any four. Achieving a united Ireland was listed as one of the top four by 15% in 2022 and 22% in 2023. Preparing for it was listed by 12% and 20%, respectively.[23] These figures do show an increase in interest, but nonetheless the unity questions are still among the lowest priorities of Southern voters.

This is normal politics: most citizens in democracies do not spend a great deal of time thinking about abstract propositions. An interesting parallel here is with how West Germans thought about reunification with the German Democratic Republic (GDR) in the East. In the first two decades after the country was divided, ending partition was a big issue for people in the West: in 1955, in 1960 and in 1965 more than one-third of the respondents named reunification as the most important issue to be addressed in the Federal Republic. But this percentage dropped to a little over ten percentage points in 1970 and to just about two points in 1981. Even in the immediate aftermath of the fall of the Berlin Wall and less than a year before Germany was actually unified, 'asked to look 10 years ahead, only 34 percent of all respondents envisioned a unified state, while 42 percent foresaw a confederation and another 21 percent pictured two independent states as before'.[24]

AND HAVE YOU EVER THOUGHT ABOUT HOW YOU MIGHT VOTE IN THE EVENT OF A BORDER POLL?

West Germans, in other words, were strongly in favour of unification in principle but less inclined to prioritise it as the existence of the two states became an established reality, and then quite uncertain about what it should look like even as it became a live probability. This is not unlike the situation with Southern opinion about a united Ireland. It is only when the proposition becomes real that most people will start to turn a general aspiration into a concrete decision. It is at that point that the 'terms and conditions' will come into play.

Admittedly, this parallel is not exact, since East Germany was simply absorbed into the Federal Republic and its existing flags, anthem and emblems were replaced by those already in use by the West. But in the Irish case, there is also much more time to prepare than Germany, faced with the implosion of the GDR, was given.

In the deliberative forum that tested the views of Southerners, the issue of national symbols was 'particularly deeply felt and emotional' yet at least some participants 'felt that it was appropriate to have negotiations on these cultural symbols to take on board views from Northern Ireland and ensure symbolic representation for the island as a whole'.[25] Assuming a border poll is called in a responsible manner, there is no reason why consultative assemblies for seeking agreement on these issues could not be up and running – and perhaps even producing recommendations – well before voting day.

Two other considerations should be kept in mind. One is that if a new flag and anthem were agreed in principle, it would be possible to engage the public on both sides of the border in an exciting process of choosing designs and compositions. The other is that a united Ireland would surely not ban the use of either of the existing flags or anthems. Most of the occasions on which people sing the anthems are not official state ceremonies – they are, in particular, sporting events. Is anyone going to ban the singing of 'Amhrán na bhFiann' or the waving of the tricolour at Croke Park? Certainly not. The adoption of new symbols for a new Ireland would not preclude continuing respect for the old emblems of either Irishness or Britishness.

The case for a united Ireland

As for the larger question of whether Southerners would be prepared to agree to the continuation of a Belfast-based devolved administration after the transfer of sovereignty from the UK to Ireland, the evidence of reluctance should not be taken as definitive. Asked in the 2024 ARINS/*The Irish Times* survey whether 'consideration should be given to significant changes to the existing political institutions' in the event of Irish unity, 58% of respondents in the Republic said they agree or strongly agree, with just 16% disagreeing.[26] People, it seems, may be reluctant to consent at this stage to specific large-scale changes in the way Ireland would be governed after unification – but they know change would have to happen.

Again, as with flags and emblems, the issue will look very different in the context of a concrete proposition on unification than in the abstract. First, it is important to note that most Southerners understand very well that unity would require large-scale constitutional change. In the 2023 ARINS/*The Irish Times* survey, only a fifth (21%) of respondents in the Republic said they would opt to keep the Constitution of Ireland unchanged in the event of unity. (This would not in fact be possible, but this answer gives a good indication of the limited extent of conservatism on the issue.) Thirty per cent would amend the existing Constitution to facilitate the changes necessary for unification. And the largest group – 35% – would favour the creation of a whole new Constitution for the island.[27] Thus over two-thirds of Southerners are prepared for constitutional change. And it should be remembered that when faced with radical constitutional change in an uplifting political context – the rewriting of Articles 2 and 3 in support of the Belfast Agreement in 1998 – voters in the Republic overwhelmingly embraced the opportunity.

Second, the continuation of a devolved administration in Belfast need not be taken in isolation. It could be an opportunity for the Republic to deal with one of the great structural weaknesses in its own democracy: the over-centralisation of government.

In October 2023, the Congress of Local and Regional Authorities – the pan-European political assembly representing local and regional authorities from the 46 member states of the

Council of Europe – issued a damning report on local government in Ireland. It noted that 'in many respects the position of local government is weaker in Ireland than in most other European countries. It has a more limited set of functions, represents a smaller share of public affairs, and can only marginally influence the size of its resources.'[28] Irish local authorities have minimal ability to make democratic decisions, with the report highlighting the way an imbalance in power between elected councillors and appointed chief executives in local authorities creates a democratic deficit. While local authorities in the EU account on average for 23% of public spending, in Ireland the equivalent figure is just 8%.

This is one of the biggest barriers to the effective functioning of the state. Irish culture is intensely local and much of its energy derives from this sense of place. But participation in decision-making at a local level is deliberately crushed by the present obsessively centralised system of government. This, then, presents an enormous opportunity in the context of a united Ireland. The devolution of powers to Belfast could be extended (albeit in somewhat different ways) to Galway, Cork, Sligo, Waterford – and indeed to Dublin itself, which does not currently even have a directly elected mayor. Placed in the context of a much broader return of democratic decision-making to local and regional authorities across the island, the continued existence of a devolved administration in Belfast might look very different to Southern voters.

This, nonetheless, leaves us with the most important questions for Southern voters: will a united Ireland be peaceful and will it cost them too much?

Will there be violence?

The honest answer is that no one can say. It is reasonable to assume that some loyalist paramilitary groups would try to use terror tactics to disrupt the process of unification either before a border poll (if they thought their side was going to lose) or after. But four questions would determine how serious such a threat would be.

First, would most of the Protestant/unionist population support violent resistance? There is no evidence that it would, especially if the leadership of political unionism honours its commitments to respect the democratic decision of the people of Northern Ireland. We know that terrorist campaigns are extremely difficult to sustain without significant levels of active support (hiding or transporting weapons, providing intelligence and safe houses) and passive tolerance (refusing to tell the authorities about suspicious movements). It is not at all obvious that a loyalist campaign would have what Mao Zedong, in describing the conditions necessary for a guerrilla army, called the sea for the fish to swim in.

Second, how well prepared would unification be? There is no doubt that a precipitous and badly planned move to a united Ireland would risk serious conflict. But there is a widespread understanding at governmental level in Dublin and London and among most political actors in the Republic and in Northern nationalism that it would be a terrible idea to spring a border poll with a simplistic proposition and a 50% plus one threshold on the twin electorates. A deep process of engagement and negotiation would surely precede unification. This process would not conciliate those who are inclined to violence, but it would considerably lessen the sense of coercion and help to create a calmer atmosphere in which most people would accept the results, even if they were not to their liking.

Third, what kind of security arrangements would be put in place? It is not credible to think that the Irish authorities would be so naive as to expect to have the Garda Síochána patrolling on the Shankill Road the day after unification. Nor is it likely that the British authorities – who after all would have a continuing interest in the maintenance of peace – would simply abandon their security responsibilities. The precise arrangements would be a delicate matter and there might have to be a significant period of transition, but there is no reason in principle why they could not be put in place.

Fourth, what have loyalists and militant unionists done in the past? There is a long history of threatening violence in response to political changes, from the Anglo-Irish Agreement in 1985 to the Northern Ireland Protocol in 2021. Graffiti signed by the Protestant Action Force (PAF) – a cover name previously used by the UVF and UDA – threatened war over the Northern Ireland Protocol in 2022.[29] They amounted to very little in the end. It would be foolish to be complacent about such threats, but perhaps equally so to assume that there is or would be the capacity to carry them out.

What are the economic prospects?

Before we can think about how much unification might cost ordinary people in the South, we have to consider two things. Would unification in itself bring economic growth? And how generous would Britain be in facilitating the process?

A critical point in relation to the estimates of a €20 billion-per-year price tag for unification put forward by FitzGerald and Morgenroth (see Chapter 1) is that they themselves acknowledged that 'Throughout this note no account is taken of the wider economic effects of Irish unification, effects which would themselves have major implications for the public finances in both parts of the island.'[30] We therefore have to imagine what those wider effects might be. If unification in itself made the all-island economy bigger, the balance between costs and benefits would look very different.

One thing we can say with confidence is that politics affects economics. Cross-border trade in goods and services was estimated in March 2024 to be valued at approximately €11.6 billion. This was a threefold increase since the Belfast Agreement in 1998.[31] And just as the Agreement created conditions in which cross-border trade could grow, so did Brexit.

Brexit showed that the two parts of Ireland were already far too intertwined for a hard border to be possible. The border has become too porous. It may be true that most Southerners do not have strong personal connections in the North, but there is nonetheless constant movement between the two jurisdictions simply as part of daily economic life.

The current evidence suggests that there were almost 50 million road traffic border crossings in 2023, with a further million train journeys between Belfast and Dublin. About 18,000 people commuted across the border to work. (About 40% of them work in public services, particularly healthcare and education.) There were 4,000 cross-border third-level students and 2,400 first- and second-level pupils crossing the border from the North, and a currently unknown number of pre-third-level students travelling in the opposite direction. The number working or studying across the border therefore totalled a minimum of 25,000 people in 2023 – though this is almost certainly an underestimate since it does not include those working in more casual jobs, especially in construction.[32]

Goods, too, flow across the border. In 2021, approximately 35% of Northern Ireland's imports (€2.6 billion) came from the Republic and 53% of its exports went to Ireland (€5.6 billion).[33] (Goods moving between Northern Ireland and Great Britain are not included in these figures as they are counted as internal trade.) While sales to and purchases from Great Britain account for the largest proportion of Northern Ireland's trade, another of the ironies of Brexit is that it has led to an increase in cross-border commerce. The current patterns suggest that this trade will continue to grow and will be significantly stronger by the time of any border poll.

But there are huge opportunities for further growth. At the moment, cross-border trade in services is much lower than that in goods. Firms in both the North and the South are more likely to export services to Great Britain than they are to sell them across the border. Services make up 26% of the total trade going from Northern Ireland to the Republic and 16% of the trade going from Ireland to Northern Ireland.[34] This is strikingly low because services make up about half of Ireland's total exports. A coordinated all-island approach to such trade would almost certainly generate more growth in services, more jobs and more tax revenue.

The evidence suggests that increasing cross-border trade can be a virtuous circle. InterTrade Ireland's research shows that 'firms that trade across the Border tend to be more resilient and innovative and generally outperform their non-exporting peers'.[35]

One-third of cross-border traders reported increased sales compared with one-quarter of those that do not sell across the border; and three-quarters of businesses with cross-border sales said they were profitable, compared with two-thirds of those that do not sell across the border.

Moreover, the experience of trading across the border encourages businesses to develop other export markets too. Those that sell across the island go on to sell off the island as well. In other words, the more cross-border trade there is, the more innovative, profitable and export-oriented firms there will be.

An all-island economy would have greater economies of scale and more efficiency in investment in infrastructure – particularly in the transition to a carbon-free economy. (The only port on the island currently capable of supporting large-scale offshore wind farms is Belfast.) If a high-speed Cork–Dublin–Belfast rail corridor were properly developed, it would also have the critical mass of skills and population to attract greater foreign direct investment. If the tax and welfare systems were the same for the whole island, it would be far easier than it is now for workers to move jobs and seek out better opportunities. All these factors create the strong possibility that unification would not simply put the two economies together – the new whole would be greater than the sum of its parts.

What would Britain do?

A central question for the financing of Irish unification is whether Britain would continue for an extended period to pay pensions in Northern Ireland and whether it would assume responsibility for Northern Ireland's share of the UK's national debt. The pessimistic assessment of these possibilities is laid out in Chapter 1. But there are reasons to assume that British attitudes would be more benign.

The most salient of these is that Irish unification would not be a one-sided process. Under the Belfast Agreement, London is just as heavily committed to facilitating it as Dublin is. Honouring the

The case for a united Ireland

democratically expressed wishes of the people of Northern Ireland is a joint responsibility.

What we're talking about, then, is not annexation or coerced separation. It is a consensual process of transferring sovereignty from one friendly state to another.

Britain's international reputation would be on the line. Its desire for closer relations with the EU would also be in play – the evidence from the Brexit crisis is that the EU takes very seriously its own sense of obligation towards the peace process in Ireland. It is also reasonable to assume that any US administration would expect Britain to be generous and constructive in its approach to Irish unification. And we should not underestimate the feeling in Britain itself that the end of partition would be a moment at which it could finally be reconciled with one of the most difficult parts of its own history – its unhappy relationship with Ireland.

Self-interest would also be at work. Britain would not want to have on its doorstep an unstable Ireland with all the possibilities for conflict that it knows from recent history. And Britain would also be improving its own long-term finances simply by being relieved of the burden of its annual subsidy to Northern Ireland – money that could eventually go towards tackling the dire regional inequalities in Britain itself. There is every reason to think that Britain would want to see the final solution to its Irish Question being reached as smoothly as possible.

At the very least, it is hard to imagine circumstances in which Britain would not be willing to continue to pay the pensions of those who have served directly in Northern Ireland: military veterans, retired police, senior public servants. How far such willingness would extend and how long it would last would be matters for negotiation. But it is not at all fanciful to imagine that, in an atmosphere of goodwill and reconciliation generated by the historic nature of the handing over of sovereignty, it could be wide and reasonably long. The obvious period of time would simply be the lifetimes of the current pensioners.

In relation to the national debt, the precedent of the Irish Free State agreeing to assume its proportion in 1922 cuts both ways.

Yes, it did – and yes, Britain then forgave that debt in 1925 for purely political reasons. In relation to the other precedent – the willingness of the Scottish government to assume its share of the debt if it won the independence referendum in 2014 – things are not so straightforward either.

The obvious reality is that Northern Ireland's place in the UK is not the same as Scotland's. The UK did not create Scotland, which is a very old political entity. It did create Northern Ireland. And its relationship to it has been, to put it mildly, vastly more conflicted. If proof were needed that the UK is prepared to treat Northern Ireland very differently to Scotland, we need look no further than Brexit – there is no such thing as the Scottish Protocol to the withdrawal agreement.

One other point about the debt is relevant. If the UK did agree to accept responsibility for Northern Ireland's share, this would not only mean that Ireland's public finances would not be damaged. They would actually improve. A state's creditworthiness – and its interest payments – is calibrated according to the ratio of debt to GDP. Irish GDP would expand automatically through unification, but in this scenario its national debt would not rise. Hence the debt-to-GDP ratio would actually fall and borrowing would become cheaper.

What happens to social welfare?

There is no doubt that the two social welfare systems have diverged radically in this century, with far more means-tested benefits in the North and far higher universal payments in the South. A new system would have to be designed – but this would be an opportunity as well as a challenge. The fact is that both jurisdictions have fundamental problems of poverty. In the North, 18% of individuals (approximately 349,000 people) were estimated to be living in relative poverty in 2022–3.[36] A quarter of children were in relative poverty. In the Republic, 12.5% of individuals and 15.0% of children were at risk of poverty in the same period.

Arguably, both systems have failed, in different ways. Between 2004 and 2023, income poverty for children was always higher in the North than in the South. But the higher cost of living in the Republic means that material deprivation for children has been worse in the South than in the North. In Northern Ireland, the two-child limit in UK welfare policy has been 'a major driver of child poverty'.[37] In the Republic, the absence of a second rate of child benefit targeted at those most in need has kept around 40,000 children in poverty.

What this suggests is that both of the current systems have strengths and both have very considerable weaknesses. Some of the North's means-tested benefits are more effective than the South's system of payments. But the absence of a two-child limit in the South makes its system in other respects more decent and humane. The process of unification ought to include a rigorous assessment of what works best for families and children and what ought to be ditched because it is either too ineffective, too cruel, or both. The point is that while creating a new all-island welfare system would certainly be an onerous task, it could also be one that results in better supports for those who need them most.

What would the health service look like?

We know from all the survey evidence that healthcare is very high on the list of concerns that most people have about a united Ireland. But we also know that most people in the Republic are deeply unhappy with their current system. In a 2024 study involving approximately 46,000 respondents across 23 European countries, fewer than two in five adults in Ireland (39%) said they were satisfied with their country's healthcare system – 6% very satisfied, and 33% quite satisfied. This puts Ireland towards the bottom of the international rankings: the European average for satisfaction was 56%. Fifty-two per cent of Irish adults said they had issues getting a hospital bed, more than twice the European average (25%). And – significantly in the context of unification

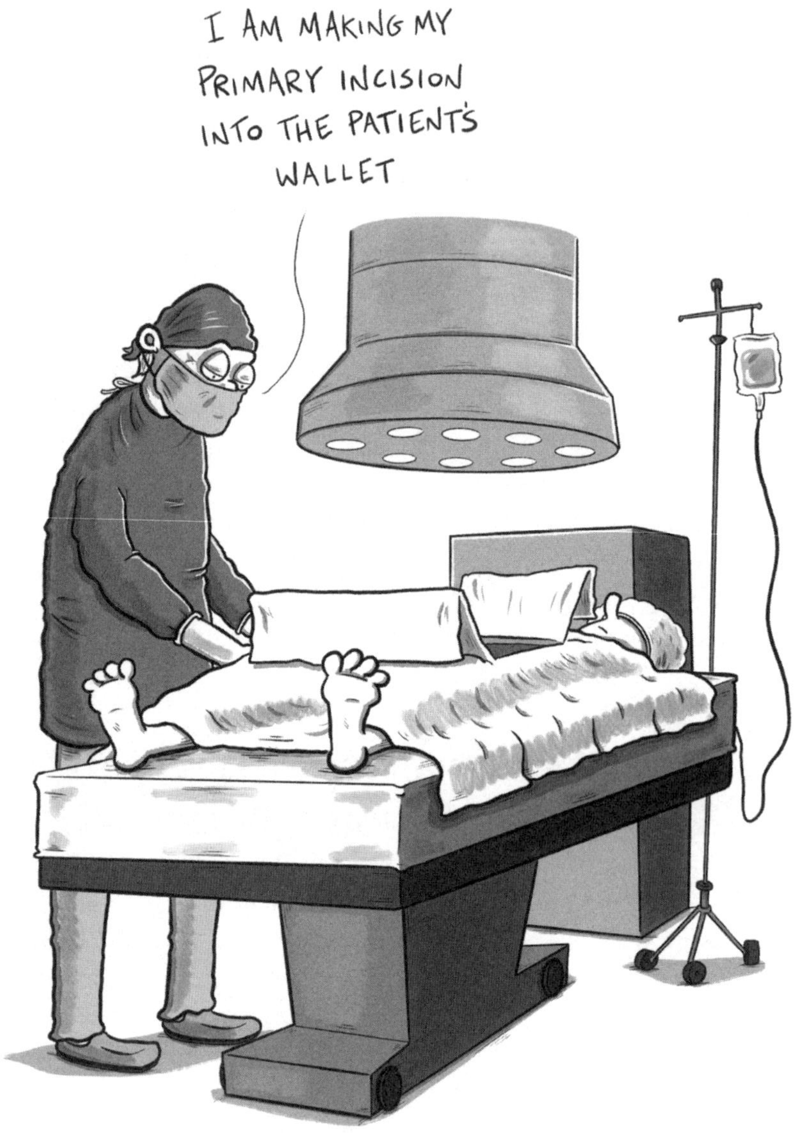
I AM MAKING MY PRIMARY INCISION INTO THE PATIENT'S WALLET

– just over half of Irish adults (52%) declared themselves willing to pay more for a better health service, well above the European average of 42%.[38]

What this tells us is that most people in the Republic are not happy with its current healthcare system and that there is a strong appetite for something better. It is also true that long-term development in the South is towards something much more like the NHS in the North. The Sláintecare plan, which has the support of all parties and forms the template for policy reforms, envisages 'a universal health and social care system where everyone has equitable access to services based on need and not the ability to pay'.[39] The Public Only Consultant Contract, which commenced in March 2023, has gone some distance towards disentangling the public from the private hospital system. As a result of the expansion of eligibility measures – including free GP (general practioner) care for those aged under 8 and over 70 and for people earning no more than the median household income – more than half the population is now eligible for either a medical or a GP visit card. (It is notable that there has been a pattern in recent years of GPs leaving the NHS in the North to work in the South.[40])

This progress has been slow and uneven but there is no doubt about the direction of travel – both parts of the island will have, at least in principle, an NHS-style system. It is certainly true that the very heavy presence of private health insurance in the Republic would be difficult to erase in the context of unification. A parallel private system may well be a reality that has to be lived with for a considerable period after the disappearance of the border. But it should be borne in mind that 'prominent motivators for having health insurance' include 'the perceived inadequacies of the public health system and the belief that services can be accessed quicker through health insurance'. Over half of all adults agree that having health insurance 'means always getting a better level of health care service' and that 'having health insurance means you can skip the queues'.[41] The corollary, however, is that if there were universal and equitable access to an adequate public system, demand for private insurance would drop substantially over time.

As with so many other questions relating to unification, the answer depends on a serious commitment to long-term planning. This may present a formidable challenge, but the good news is that most of this planning has to be done anyway. Even if unity were off the table, the Republic would have to be moving consistently towards an NHS-type healthcare system – and the roadmap (Sláintecare) is already agreed. Implementing that plan is indeed critical to the prospects for unity – but it is also an internal political imperative for Irish governments. If, by 2030, the Republic has the universal and equitable healthcare system it has promised itself, there will be a much more convincing answer to Northern concerns about what would happen to the NHS in the event of unification.

What happens to education?

There is no doubt that, as things stand, a united Ireland would inherit a patchwork of primary and secondary school types. Nor is there much room for argument about the size of the task involved in bringing educational attainment – and therefore economic productivity – in the North up to the standards of the South. But both of these difficulties also represent opportunities.

Both jurisdictions have education systems that were shaped in large measure by struggles for control between secular and religious forces. Both are shaped by the legacies of sectarianism, which are starkly obvious in the North's divides between Catholic and state schools but increasingly so also in the South's mismatch between an overwhelmingly Catholic system on the one hand and a religiously diverse population on the other. In both jurisdictions, anachronistic systems are kept in place largely by inertia. The process of unification could provide the energy needed for a reshaping and modernisation of educational provision. As with healthcare, much of this change has to happen anyway – neither system of provision is currently fit for purpose. Thinking about reform in an all-island context can help to clarify and refocus both education systems on

The case for a united Ireland

the fundamental question of how all children, regardless of their family backgrounds, can be assured equal access to excellent schools.

On the broader question of education and productivity, it is interesting that the dynamic here is the opposite of that in healthcare. In health, the need is to make the South's system more like the North's. In education, it works the other way around. For all its many faults, the Republic's system has been much better than that in the North at providing equality of opportunity – especially the opportunity for working-class kids to move from second to third level.

As John FitzGerald has put it: 'If Northern Ireland immediately reformed its educational system to provide genuine equality of opportunity, after 20 to 30 years, as the children who are currently being failed progress through the educational system, there would be a big impact on productivity in Northern Ireland, as happened in this part of the island once we improved our educational system. It took 30 years, from 1970 to the mid-1990s.'[42]

FitzGerald put his finger on one of the big barriers to this kind of change: the selective system that operates in the North may leave far too many working-class children behind, but it benefits middle-class families. He poses a purposely awkward question: 'If we unify and the education system in Northern Ireland has not been reformed, do we immediately force the Irish system on Northern Ireland? I know that would be very unpopular with middle-class nationalists as well as people of a unionist background. Alternatively, do we leave it where it stands whereby there is an ethos that does not believe in equality of opportunity and does not look after kids from disadvantaged backgrounds in Northern Ireland?'[43]

But if we stand back from this question, we can also see that it doesn't just present a problem. It illuminates the possibility of an immense benefit for the very people who may currently be seen as those most likely to be bitterly opposed to unification: working-class Protestants, especially boys. This has long been recognised not just as a social and economic problem, but as a political issue for the peace process. The New Decade, New Approach deal that led to the restoration of the Northern Ireland Executive and Assembly following three years of political stalemate included a commitment to create a plan 'to address links between persistent educational underachievement and socio-economic background, including the longstanding issues facing working-class, Protestant boys'.[44]

Yet there is little evidence that Northern Ireland's own institutions are capable of dealing with this 'persistent' failure. The Republic, on the other hand, can point to the very considerable evidence that it has been much more successful in creating educational opportunity for children from poorer backgrounds – with hugely benign consequences for individuals, for society and for economic productivity. To turn around FitzGerald's question, the imposition of a fairer educational system might be unpopular with both Catholic and Protestant middle-class families – but would it not therefore be rather popular in working-class communities, especially the very Protestant communities who most need to be persuaded that a united Ireland could work in their interests?

Conclusion

The case for a united Ireland is highly problematic – but only if we think of unification as an event rather than a process. This is, admittedly, the way it is framed by the Belfast Agreement: a border poll is called, the nationalist side wins by however narrow a margin, and Ireland is one country. But that is neither a likely nor a desirable scenario. Ireland is not Germany in 1990, where one state is rapidly falling apart and the other has to move very quickly to absorb it. Nor is Northern Ireland like, say, Kosovo violently breaking away from Serbia in 1998. Its separation from the United Kingdom will be consensual – and the UK will remain centrally involved in a process it is pledged to facilitate. There would be a range of governmental actors – Dublin, London, Brussels and perhaps (depending on the long-term effects of the second Trump administration) Washington – working together to ease the process.

The difference between an event and a process is that a process is dynamic. Its effects are cumulative and they can create their own momentum. Posed in the abstract, questions of symbolism are difficult to answer and citizens on both sides of the border are more likely to cling to what they already know. But faced with a concrete possibility of unification, they will begin to think actively about pros and cons, to weigh up costs and benefits and to gauge the familiar things they might lose against the new things they might gain.

The great advantage of planning seriously for the possibility of a united Ireland is that most of what needs to be done to prepare for it is good for everyone whether unification happens or not. Strengthening cross-border trade generates greater prosperity and helps companies to grow. Learning and adopting what works best in the two welfare systems makes both of them better at lifting people out of poverty. Creating a fair and efficient health service in the Republic doesn't just make it easier to fuse with the NHS, it addresses one of the biggest concerns that most of its citizens currently have about their own state's public provision. Ending the disproportionate religious control of education on both sides of the border and ending Northern Ireland's socially discriminatory system are proper goals for their own sakes, as well as being steps on the way to unity.

This is what will make a united Ireland attractive not just as an idea or an aspiration, but as a process of tangible improvement in the daily lives of all who share the island. It can become not the fulfilment of an ancient historic destiny but the stimulus to create a more prosperous, sustainable and socially just future.

4.
The case against a united Ireland

SAM McBRIDE

A lot to lose

Whether we loathe the partition of Ireland or hope that it will endure, the border is firmly embedded in the lives of the island's people in innumerable ways. Most of the ways in which the border manifests itself now seem so natural that many people do not even consciously recognise them as stemming from the decision of those who in 1921 drew a wiggly line around the six north-eastern counties.

North of that border, Northern Ireland is a highly integrated part of one of the world's top economies and one of the great civilisations, which gave birth to the most significant language in human history. The Union's influence is daily evident in the lives of Northern Irish citizens, from the significant (the currency they spend and the dominant east–west trade route) to the mundane (listening to the BBC while travelling roads marked in miles).

South of that border, the Republic of Ireland is one of the world's most successful small nations. It is astonishingly wealthy, has warm relations with all its neighbours and influence with the world's dominant superpower that is unprecedented for a country of its size. After past animosity, some of which stemmed from well-intentioned but impossible dreams, North–South relations on the island of Ireland have matured into sensible cooperation that recognises a shared inheritance and challenges while respecting that the two parts of the island are different.

Alluring as some of the arguments for Irish unity might be, they involve the insurmountable risk of abandoning a situation that has been getting progressively better.

If leaving the EU – a club of sovereign nations – was messy for the UK after a few decades, then taking Northern Ireland's six counties out of the UK after hundreds of years of integration will unquestionably be far more difficult.

The paradox of Brexit is that it has made a referendum on Irish unity more possible than ever before, yet it has simultaneously made it harder for nationalism to win such a plebiscite. Many people have only thought shallowly about a united Ireland. They have busy lives and don't want to absorb complex detail about something that doesn't seem imminent.

Yet regardless of whether a referendum is ever held, there is now real debate about the topic. As ferociously divided as Britain became over leaving the EU, Remainers were never going to set off bombs in London. Here, violence is a serious risk if this referendum is bungled. For that reason, we have a solemn responsibility in how we consider this issue. Lives may depend on our decision. This process involves different considerations for each of us, depending on which side of the border we sit. But regardless of where we are, everyone on this island has a stake in the outcome. If Irish unity happens, it is in all our interests to make the greatest possible success of it. If it doesn't happen, it is in all our interests to make the greatest possible success of both Northern Ireland and the Republic of Ireland.

An inheritance of strife

In Ireland, we have both too much history and too little. We are weighed down by centuries of stories recounting atrocities in which our ancestors were either victims or perpetrators. Yet we know too little of the richness of history's complexity. A partial folk history is handed down in which the wrongs of one's ancestors are minimised and the butchery of one's opponents is amplified. It's not fiction, but it's partial. Even for those who think they've little interest in or knowledge of history, it infects their thinking because it is absorbed from family, from separate schools, from differing media, and from the myriad marks of division that stain Northern society in particular.

Karl Marx once observed that 'men make their own history, but they do not make it as they please; they do not make it under self-selected circumstances … the tradition of all dead generations weighs like a nightmare on the brains of the living'.[1] You don't have to be a Marxist to appreciate the wisdom of those words. Yet many today believe that we are beyond repeating the sins of our forebears. In that hubris lies acute danger. Irish history is replete with cycles of atrocity followed by peace; once past the atrocity, there is often the belief that what has happened is too terrible to ever recur – but it does.

One of the most disconcerting elements of the outbreak of the Troubles is how many intelligent people had decided Northern Ireland was beyond such violence. In November 1968, after the infamous RUC attack on a civil rights march in Londonderry, the distinguished liberal unionist editor of the *Belfast Telegraph*, Jack Sayers, viewed the protest as part of 'the diminishing Irish volcano', which, he said, 'has had an eruption, but something says it could be one of the last'.[2]

He was far from alone. SDLP founding member Paddy Devlin recalled of the 1960s that 'for the first time in 40 years there was a spirit of compromise in the air. People from the two communities were more prepared than ever before to live together in harmony.'[3] Yet a terrible murderous force was about to be released, feeding on pent-up hatreds that had been there all along, but to which even many perceptive observers had been blind.

Writing in 1977 as the Troubles raged around him, Belfast historian A.T.Q. Stewart remarked that 'significantly, the act of triggering the seismic catastrophe in Northern Ireland was carried out by a generation too young to have any possible realisation of the nature and consequences of previous Irish troubles'.[4]

Today, we face an additional challenge. One in five of the Republic's population was born outside its borders (19% in 2022, and there's been massive inward migration since then),[5] and Northern Ireland has a population of more than 13% born outside its borders.[6] In both jurisdictions, migration is likely to rise over coming decades due to a declining birthrate, an ageing population and our relative global wealth.

These people have not just the right to take part in this debate, but the responsibility to do so because they, like everyone else, will share in the consequences, for good or ill. They will be free of the shackles of history that cling to those of us whose ancestors have lived here for centuries. But that freedom hides the danger of ignorance about the forces that have shaped this island and have meant that, in the words of Stewart, 'there can hardly be a square inch of earth anywhere in Ireland that has not been at some time stained with blood'.[7]

A union that has stubbornly endured

The United Kingdom of Great Britain and Northern Ireland is not just a legal and political union, but a historically rich union of trade, culture, security, identity and outlook. Though a union of diverse peoples, it encapsulates shared heritage, while affording equal privileges.

English, and then British, control of Ireland stems from at least Tudor times. It has involved enforced plantation of settlers, bloody conquest and gruesome atrocities. When Queen Elizabeth II made her seminal speech in Dublin Castle in 2011, she was being exceptionally euphemistic in her regret when she said: 'With the benefit of historical hindsight we can all see things which we would wish had been done differently or not at all.'[8]

The Plantation of Ulster was brutal. The Act of Union was secured by bribes. Catholics (and, for a long time, dissenting Protestants) were harshly repressed. But accepting all of those facts does not necessitate support for ending the Union, any more than the acceptance of the brutality of the North American colonies and ensuing slavery necessitates support for the breakup of the US.

We must deal with the world as we find it. We cannot be held accountable for what our long-dead forefathers did. Regardless of how things got to be how they are, the only logical test can be: would they be better or worse if changed?

Often proponents of breaking up the Union resort to what seem like self-evident truths that are nothing of the sort. They see the plantation of Ulster as a barbaric imposition on the native Irish, yet find it acceptable that white Europeans should drive Native Americans off their land and butcher them when they objected.

Indeed, Irish Americans ferociously opposed to the partition of Ireland now live in the land taken from another people.

As the writer Dervla Murphy observed in the 1970s: 'It helps to remember that the Protestants have been in Northern Ireland longer than the whites have been in the US. It *is* now their country as much as Catholics'; they have no other. Had the Gaels been "subdued" as effectively as the Red Indians and the Aboriginals there would be no disputing that point.'[9] Others see it as geographically self-evident that an island should be one nation – yet support Scottish independence, which would partition our neighbouring island.

Even those who engage in centuries-old grievance-mongering only want to go back so far. They don't, for instance, want Ireland to be held responsible for the marauding attacks launched on Britain from this island as the Romans' grip weakened. Nor do many who now pin British colonialism on today's UK feel any need for repentance over Irish colonialism in Britain when in the fourth and fifth centuries large Irish-speaking colonies were established in south-west Wales. Cormac, bishop of Cashel, recorded how 'the power of the Irish over the Britons was great, and they had divided Britain between them into estates … as far as the English channel'.[10]

The Union we now know was born in compromise and has evolved in compromise. Any union – whether a political union, a trade union or a marriage union – involves give and take. Staying in such a union doesn't imply perfection but demonstrates the belief that the sum of that union's parts is greater than they would be apart and that the Union is an effective means to reconcile competing demands and allegiances across four nations.

The United Kingdom has developed in ways that would once have been unimaginable yet were provided for by the absence of a codified constitution, allowing for flexibility through custom and practice, which is easier to alter than law. This political union forged the British Empire on which the sun never set – an empire in which Irishmen of all faiths played a full and enthusiastic role and in which some of the most brutal colonial enforcers were

The case against a united Ireland

Catholic Irishmen, an awkward reality for those who see Ireland as simply a victim of Britain.

It was also the Union that stood lonely against Hitler when Ireland was neutral and the US refused to defend the world from a uniquely evil tyrant. Northern Ireland played a proud role in the defeat of the Nazis. Conscription never applied on this island, meaning that every one of the 133,000 or so Irishmen who fought – many of them from south of the border – did so as a volunteer.

Much of the naval armada that began the liberation of Europe on D-Day assembled in Belfast Lough in spring 1944. Supreme allied commander General Dwight Eisenhower met his Irish-born deputy, General Bernard Montgomery, in Omagh to plan the assault on the Nazis' Atlantic Wall. Eisenhower later said: 'Without Northern Ireland, I do not see how the American forces could have concentrated to begin the invasion of Europe.'[11] On the morning of 6 June, the Royal Ulster Rifles' second battalion stormed Sword Beach near Caen while the regiment's first battalion was dropped behind enemy lines by glider.

There is shame in Northern Ireland's history. But there should also be immense pride that in humanity's darkest conflagration it was on the side of the righteous.

The Union has been extraordinarily resilient. It has survived the growth and death of empire, two world wars, the Cold War, economic upheaval, devolution, Brexit, hapless prime ministers and turmoil in the Royal Family.

It has not survived through force alone. This is a state that has for more than a century pragmatically accepted that if Northern Ireland wishes to leave, then it is free to do so.[12] Soldiers won't be sent to put down our wishes; the courts won't rule our vote unconstitutional, and we won't face persecution for wanting to depart. It's easy to forget how rare this is. The US, Spain, France and many other western nations don't accept peaceful secession for parts of their territory.

The Union is not without episodic ignominy. It was preceded by Cromwell's genocidal expedition. After the Union came the unspeakable scandal of the Famine[13] and the policy of reprisals during the Irish War of Independence, in which innocent civilians were slaughtered to send a message to the IRA.

This is inexcusable and abhorrent. But if on this island he without sin were to cast the first stone, then no stones would be cast by any side. These shameful episodes deserve to be remembered, to be understood and to serve as a warning to us as to where hatred can lead. But they are not a sensible basis on which to form or not form a new country.

We must deal with the circumstances we have inherited; we cannot undo past injustices. Moreover, a naive attempt to do so could lead not to a form of justice, but to those already dead being joined in the cold earth by another generation of the slain.

Partition as a pragmatic compromise

The Union has from the outset been immensely flexible. It incorporates a single armed forces with military units bearing distinct regional attributes. It is a unitary state, yet each of the four nations that make up the UK has its own football team. It has a central parliament but also devolved executives in Cardiff, Edinburgh and Belfast. It is an unusually adaptable constitutional arrangement.

In many ways, the partition of Ireland followed this pattern of iterative flexibility. No one got all they desired. But enough people got enough of what they wanted to be able to live with the result. It is easy to decry partition based on what we now know: the discrimination against Northern Catholics, the Church-dominated insular Southern state, the economic regression of the North, the continuation of sectarianism, and manifold problems we know too well.

But just as the Good Friday Agreement was imperfect yet had a sound logical basis, so the creation of the border happened for reasons we should now be careful to judge. Had there not been compelling logic to that decision, and had the Anglo-Irish Treaty not commanded the support that it did, partition could not have happened, far less endured.

The case against a united Ireland

Faced with the alternative of bloody civil war triggered by unionists who felt abandoned, the creation of two self-governing jurisdictions was intended as a stopgap. The fact it has lasted for over a century and there is no immediate prospect of the border being removed is a powerful testament to the utility of this solution. It has worked, after a fashion. People work and love and live their lives, for the most part in peace and prosperity that would have been alien to our ancestors. Demonstrably, partition remains problematic. But the alternatives could be worse, and many of the practical problems of infrastructure and services across the border can be managed through the all-island architecture of the Agreement.

In the Republic, it is increasingly difficult to argue that partition is seriously damaging. The economy has boomed. Where the Irish once poured out in search of work, migrants now pour in. The Northern violence that once threatened to spill across the border has gone. Relations with both Northern Ireland and the UK are strong. Irish self-confidence has soared. Truly, Ireland has taken its place among the nations of the earth in politics, in business and in sport.

The basis for this is, however, fragile. The Agreement states that once 50% plus one – the narrowest possible majority – of Northern Ireland's citizens want Irish unity, that must happen, so long as Southern voters agree. In truth, this has always been the pillar on which Northern Ireland rested. No state can exist where a majority of its inhabitants wish otherwise. If the slenderest of majorities votes for a united Ireland, based on both law and logic, that must happen. Yet a slim majority either way could be disastrous.

Partition was in some ways entirely artificial. The line of the border was drawn so as to maximise territory in the new Northern state to make it viable, while ensuring that unionists retained sufficient dominance to feel secure. It was crudely sectarian, yet if there was going to be partition, it made sense to trap as few people as possible on the wrong side of that frontier.

Nevertheless, in some respects the principle of partition for the north-east of the island, if not the precise border chosen, was more natural than many people now realise. Long before the plantation of Ulster, the north-eastern counties were different. In an age when travel by sea was safer than journeying overland, they were closer to Scotland geographically, economically and linguistically. Even in Ulster mythology, the fearsome warrior Cú Chulainn fathered a son with Aífe, a Scottish warrior queen.

For much of its history, Ireland was partitioned between a multitude of kingdoms. In the Middle Ages, the kingdom of Ulaid roughly spanned the eastern half of what is now Northern Ireland – the part that today is most unionist. Thus the plantation of Ulster amplified an existing difference rather than creating it.

This isn't a uniquely unionist view. Paddy Devlin, a former IRA internee, observed that during the eighteenth and nineteenth centuries 'Belfast had developed differently from the rest of Ireland' and at times had a sense of 'superior detachment' from other Irish cities. This was economic as well as religious and cultural. It defined where the city looked not just for ideas, but for trade. It was unquestionably Irish, and in the Victorian era turned to places like Sligo for cheap unskilled Catholic labour. But it was also thoroughly British to an extent that stood out. The industries that would define the city as its growth exploded were financed by Scottish capital while consuming Scottish iron and coal.[14]

The unionist cause has historically been poorly articulated by unionists. In part, that is because the case for the status quo is generally more obvious than the case for something not yet here. It is also born out of laziness – unionism has until recently had a comfortable majority so didn't need to compete in the battle of ideas. That laziness has been influenced by the sectarian (and inaccurate) attitude that Catholics will never support the Union in significant numbers and so there's no point trying to persuade them.

For many emotional unionists, the Union is about shared national bonds. It is about not just watching great national events such as the state opening of parliament, the coronation or the Last Night of the Proms, but being a part of those occasions. It is about a flag in which Northern Ireland is represented by the Cross of St Patrick, by a parliament in which the harps and patron saint of

Irishness are quite literally carved into the fabric of the building, an army where the Irish Guards and Royal Irish Regiment are simultaneously Irish and British, and a Royal Family whose titles and standard reflect Ireland. It is a Union that ties them to the kilts, pipes and tartans of the Scots; to the choirs, poetry and castles of Wales; and to the cathedrals, palaces and literary heritage of England. It is about a fair and sophisticated legal system, a nation with two of the world's oldest universities, the world's oldest currency still in use and a state that was multinational and multicultural long before the value of such concepts was more widely recognised. It is about a nation that could take Thomas Moore's nostalgic lament for Irish national decline under British rule, 'Let Erin Remember' ('Let Erin remember the days of old/Ere her faithless sons betray'd her ... Ere the emerald gem of the western world/Was set in the crown of a stranger'), as the regimental march of the Irish Guards, and his daringly anti-imperialistic 'The Minstrel Boy' as one of the traditional tunes played by massed military bands at the Cenotaph in London on Remembrance Sunday.

An undeniable risk

If the border didn't exist, no one might now create it. But it is there, and so regardless of the rights or wrongs of how it came into being, removing it is more difficult than continuing with what we have.

Voting for unity is, empirically, a greater risk than voting to retain the status quo. Change will necessarily be less certain than what now exists. Even if every promise made was given in good faith, those making the promises might not be there to implement them. Even if they were, circumstances might make them impossible to implement. What actually is done may well be different to what voters are told will be done. And in that lies incalculable uncertainty. This can be minimised but never eradicated.

Much of the argument for Irish unity is speculative, guessing as to the form of unity that might ultimately be proposed and the implications of such choices. Voting for the status quo involves far less uncertainty. While all nations experience incremental change, the best way to understand what voting for the status quo would mean is to look around at what we have today.

As Ireland has become more and more successful, the necessity to remove the border has receded. That is expressed not just in law, where the Agreement saw the Irish constitutional claim on Northern Ireland dropped, but in purely practical terms: if the Republic is thriving as it is, why throw everything up in the air by creating an entirely new country?

Even the most churlish unionist would accept that the Republic has been a remarkable success. It wasn't for decades, but it has dramatically risen from penury to Solomonesque wealth. Those experiencing success repeatedly make the mistake of believing that it can go on forever; in fact, it often rests on fragile foundations.

A united Ireland would not mean bolting Northern Ireland on to the Republic. It would mean dismantling both states and creating an entirely new country. To remake any state would be a major risk. But on an island whose soil is saturated with centuries of bloodshed and where hundreds of thousands of Northerners do not want such an outcome, it would be a gargantuan risk. It might work. Only the most ideologically unbending would say

Where Ireland's corporation tax comes from

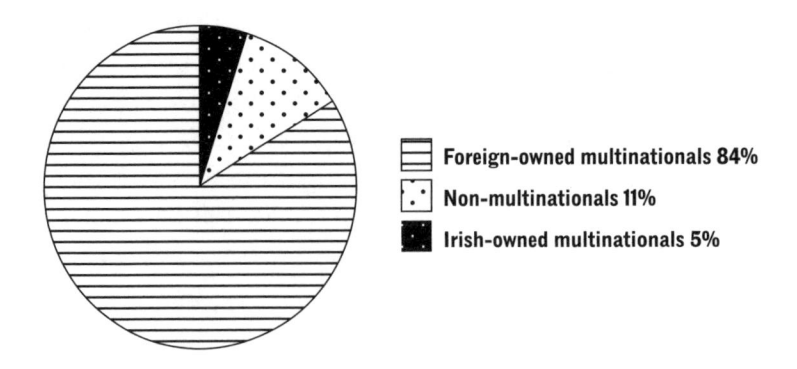

Foreign-owned multinationals 84%
Non-multinationals 11%
Irish-owned multinationals 5%

Source: Data from Irish Revenue based on 2023 payments and 2022 returns.

otherwise. But every honest exponent of Irish unity accepts that it entails risks. There are shared risks – such as the economy – and there are risks discrete to certain groups.

Long gone are the days when Joseph Murray, president of the League of Decency, could say 'I have received pledges from 2,000 people and two Protestants'[15] and Ian Paisley could say that Catholics 'breed like rabbits and multiply like vermin',[16] but the sectarianism that infects both sides remains. Indeed, one of its hallmarks is the belief by some that their side doesn't have a sectarian problem.

Unionists have reason to be sceptical of grand claims about their future treatment in a state where they will necessarily be dependent on others to ensure the fulfilment of those promises. In the early twentieth century, the unionist slogan 'Home Rule is Rome Rule' was dismissed by leading nationalists as fearmongering. Yet as the Catholic Church came to dominate much of public life, in 1949 Thomas Johnson privately told his fellow Protestant nationalist Ernest Blythe that what had happened gave credibility to the unionist slogan – something he hadn't believed at the time of the Home Rule debate.[17]

In 1978, future taoiseach Garret FitzGerald described the Republic as 'so partitionist a state that northern Protestants would be bloody fools to join it'.[18] Even Sinn Féin president Mary Lou McDonald came to accept Edward Carson's slogan, saying in 2018: 'In the south, home rule became Rome rule, just as so many unionist and Protestant people had feared and predicted. It was a cold house for Protestants, women, children and our invisible LGBT [lesbian, gay, bisexual, transgender] community.'[19]

Unionists are assured that their identities would be fully respected in a united Ireland, and many of those making such promises do so sincerely. What they are blind to, however, is the depth of anti-British sentiment that remains in Irish society. This is anti-Britishness not of the sort that would treat someone unfavourably because they have an English accent, but of the kind that in 2022 saw the removal of the inclusive wall of remembrance in Glasnevin Cemetery. It had been repeatedly vandalised with paint and sledgehammers because of the presence of the names of all those who died in the Irish Revolution. The names of British soldiers dead more than a century were so abhorrent to a section of the public that this had to be removed rather than protected. The vandals weren't representative of what is a predominantly open and welcoming society. But a handful of people couldn't achieve such a result without tapping into a deeper sentiment.

Similarly, in 2020 the Irish government abandoned an event to mark the Royal Irish Constabulary and the Dublin Metropolitan Police. The event was to commemorate – rather than celebrate or eulogise – the police forces in which thousands of Irishmen served. Yet it met with such a wave of popular and political opposition that the government abandoned its plan. The justification for this was that the notorious 'Black and Tans', an auxiliary RIC force, had engaged in war crimes during the War of Independence. That is true – yet so had both wings of the IRA. The fact that those opposing commemorating the police while lauding the IRA saw no contradiction in doing so spoke powerfully to this blindness within modern Ireland.

Many unionists also harbour some fear for how they'd be treated in a united Ireland. Not many expect to be slaughtered these days. But the memory of how the Southern Protestant population declined prior to and after partition endures. Between 1911 and 1926, that population fell by a third.[20] There were many reasons for this, but some of it was due to oppression: some overt expulsions, some involving decisions to flee after a local atrocity, some due to a boycott of their business, and some because they felt – to use David Trimble's later expression about how Northern Ireland treated Catholics – that the South had become a 'cold house' for them.

Change for the better

Significant elements of Catholic opposition to Northern Ireland were linked to structural sectarian injustice that has been removed. In fact, even before that was remedied, Catholic views of Northern

The case against a united Ireland

Ireland were more nuanced than is now commonly appreciated. In 1967, the *Belfast Telegraph* commissioned the first Northern Ireland-wide survey of opinion. Half of Catholics surveyed believed the best future involved a united Ireland linked to Britain, 20% supported the status quo, and just 30% wanted an independent united Ireland. Even allowing for the likelihood that in a unionist-dominated state some respondents said what they thought interviewers wanted to hear, those statistics show clear willingness to compromise.

At that point, nationalism didn't have a reliable unionist partner with which to deal. But Northern Ireland today is fundamentally different from the entity that existed for 77 years after partition. The difference is not only the existence of power-sharing, something that was enforced on unionism, but the broad acceptance of power-sharing. Where unionism once solidly opposed this, now only the Traditional Unionist Voice (TUV) – representing about 8% of the electorate – stands against it. And even the TUV qualifies that as being opposition to power-sharing with Sinn Féin, not the SDLP or other nationalist parties.

That is good not just for those who are Catholic and/or Irish, but for all of society. A country in which a massive proportion of the population is ill-treated might not be unsustainable, but it will never thrive by casting aside the talents of its most valuable commodity – its people.

By 2016, with power-sharing, a reformed police service incorporating many Catholic officers, and Catholics in senior positions throughout society from business to the judiciary, the Union had never been more secure. For many people, but especially for nationalists, Brexit seemed to transform this. Yet those dismayed by the UK's vote to leave the EU against the wishes of Northern Ireland often see this as an irrevocable break. Already, Britain is creeping back closer to the EU, and it may one day rejoin.

Even if that does not happen, the great nationalist fear – that Brexit would effectively repartition the island – has largely been dealt with through the Irish Sea border. It is unionists who are now bearing most of the post-Brexit constitutional pain. Brexit was a momentous decision that cannot be dismissed, yet as a journalist I know that our obsession with what's new can sometimes cloud our view of the wider landscape.

It remains the case, and will remain the case, that it is possible to live in Northern Ireland and be thoroughly Irish – to have an Irish passport, to have the state pay to educate one's children in the Irish language, to play Gaelic sports as a member of the PSNI, and to move seamlessly back and forth across the almost invisible Irish border. All of this is possible while feeling at home in Northern Ireland and climbing to the top of British life in what is a far larger country.

Michelle O'Neill embodies how the old Northern Ireland is dead and buried. When she became first minister in 2024, the highest office in the land went not to some moderate Catholic of the sort who might vote Alliance or even unionist, but to the Stormont leader of a party that doesn't want Northern Ireland to exist.

When Sinn Féin won the first minister's position in the Stormont election in 2022, there was a widespread belief that unionism wouldn't accept this. A few months earlier, the DUP had collapsed devolution over the Irish Sea border. Many nationalists believed that this was a ruse and the DUP would never accept a Sinn Féin first minister. They were wrong.

Not only did the DUP return to Stormont, but Emma Little-Pengelly embraced her position as deputy first minister with good grace, rather than attempting to rename the role 'joint first minister' or play petty games. Unionism knew it had lost fairly and squarely, it knew that rejecting democracy wasn't going to help it win back votes, and ultimately it had no realistic alternative.

Such a reality would have been unfathomable to Northern Ireland's founding fathers. Yet they made drastic and unexpected compromises of their own, most significantly when they cut loose their unionist brethren in three of Ulster's counties, having solemnly vowed in the Ulster Covenant never to do so.

From its inception, Northern Ireland has been a place of inbuilt compromise. It's imperfect to everyone, but right now it's the best way of being able to share this piece of ground without the potential for unrest whose ultimate boundaries are unknowable.

The case against a united Ireland

More than a decade ago, Gerry Adams said, 'The Orange state is gone forever.'[21] He was right. The Orange Order now struggles to get even the unionist parties to do what it wants; its influence over government policy is negligible.

But if the old Orange state that nationalists hated is gone, that recalibrates the question of Irish unity. Once, unity was the only way to get rid of the worst excesses of unionist dominance. Now there is no dominance. It's possible to have the best of both worlds: full access to the UK economically, professionally and practically, while being every bit as Irish as someone in Cork or Kerry.

Under the Northern Ireland Protocol, the protection of rights is guaranteed; even a rogue prime minister now cannot ditch these protections without triggering a likely trade war with the EU.

The economic facts of life

From a Southern perspective, there is the very real possibility that having to integrate Northern Ireland would drag down a successful society. The ending of the Troubles greatly benefited the Republic not just because of the absence of violence, but because the South could focus on normal politics. Suddenly integrating the North would consume most political and bureaucratic time.

Some 36 years after the Berlin Wall came down, Germany still hasn't managed to eradicate the economic and social divide of what was a far shorter partition in a country that didn't have Ireland's stark religious divide. Germany demonstrates that radically recreating a nation means financial pain. For those who espouse unity in the way that missionaries preach their faith, that will be a price worth paying. But those without such zeal should be aware of what's likely to be asked of them.

Sinn Féin exemplifies the denialism involved in the section of the pro-unity campaign that is akin to the Brexiteers: it wants to win at all costs and will deal with the consequences later. According to Sinn Féin, 'there is no evidence to suggest the people in the south would have to pay more taxes in the event of a united Ireland'.[22]

The precise figures can for now only be educated guesses, but it isn't credible to claim that Northern Ireland is much poorer than the South while also claiming that it can be made richer alongside having better public services and infrastructure without vast investment that ultimately will have to be paid for by Southern voters. In Germany, every taxpayer pays a tax, the *Solidaritätszuschlag*, at 5.5%. When introduced, voters were told it would be for one year. That was in 1991. It's still in place.

Northern Ireland is not a communist economy caught between two superpowers. Economically, it should be much easier to integrate. But the lesson of Germany is that such processes are rarely simpler than anticipated. Even where they largely work, multiple unforeseen difficulties emerge.

Economic pitfalls abound. On his first day as Ireland's finance minister in 1957, James Ryan was given a stark message by his top civil servant, T.K. Whitaker. The minister was warned that the survival of the state depended on the survival of its economy. Whitaker, the Rostrevor-born mandarin who reshaped economic policy away from Éamon de Valera's protectionism, told Ryan:

> In the political field the primary national objective is the reunification of the country. Until that is achieved, however, and no doubt after it has been achieved, the principal economic problem of the Irish government will continue to be the safeguarding of political independence by ensuring economic viability. Without a sound and progressive economy, political independence would be a crumbling facade.[23]

Astounding wealth has been laid on the foundations established by Whitaker and others. But wealth can take wings. The idea that Ireland's economic success is – recessionary blips notwithstanding – a permanent new reality is myopic. The re-election of Donald Trump as US president in 2024 emphasised the future uncertainty of the Republic's amazing corporate tax receipts.

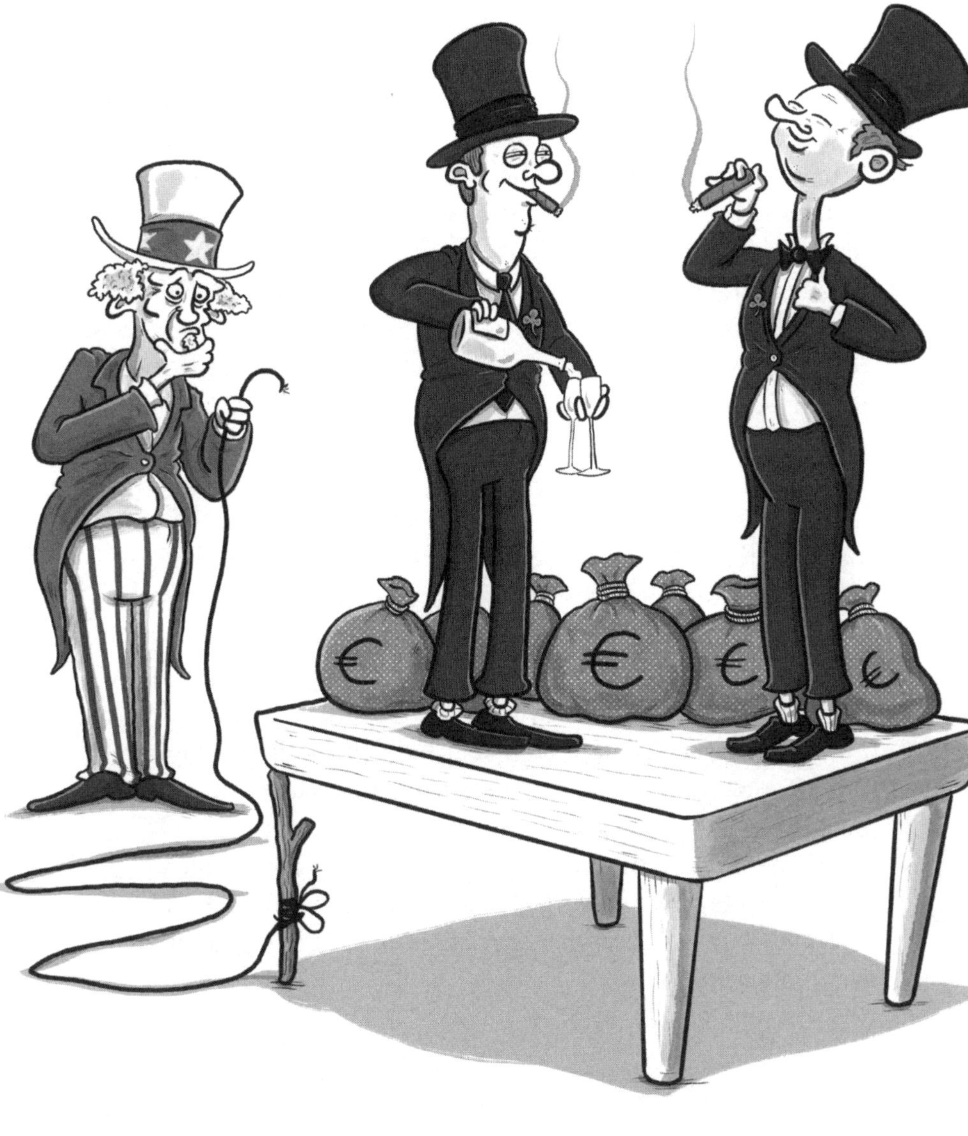

The South's wealth is founded on being a global tax haven. That policy has brought in the cash that has built roads and hospitals, bought trains, improved the education system and created a sovereign wealth fund that may one day make arguments about the South's ability to pay for the North seem absurd. But it has also undermined Irish sovereignty. Ireland is now uniquely vulnerable to the US forcing American companies to pay their taxes at home. It is vulnerable to decisions taken in US boardrooms if it suddenly suits the interests of capitalists to sway government policy this way or that.

It is also increasingly clear that Irish sovereignty isn't all that it appears. This American money comes with strings attached. When it appeared that the Oireachtas would press ahead with the Occupied Territories Bill, a law to enforce a boycott of Israeli goods made in occupied Palestinian territories, the US ambassador to Ireland wrote to the Irish government to warn that the bill could have implications for the 1,000 US firms in Ireland. US legislation prohibits American companies from complying with a foreign country's boycott unless the US approves, she told them. Some 90 minutes after the ambassador's email, the tánaiste announced that the bill would be 'reviewed'. When Trump moved to target the Irish economy with trade tariffs, the taoiseach felt the need to grin and bear Trump's ramblings while sitting in the Oval Office, terrified of upsetting the man who could decimate Ireland's economy.

All major Irish parties now support this system. Even the once avowedly left-wing Sinn Féin has told multinationals that they have nothing to fear from it. For those on the left, joining Ireland means joining an economic system built to facilitate a global tax supermarket for multinationals that isn't available to ordinary people.

It's the sort of economic success that would have appalled James Connolly. He didn't enter the General Post Office (GPO) in Easter 1916 to create a nation that specialised in facilitating tax-dodging corporate behemoths.

Radically divergent economies

It is true that the Northern Irish would have more say in a united Ireland than they have in the UK. But this cuts both ways: the English have the greatest say in the Union but they also contribute the greatest sum each year in taxation, from which Northern Ireland disproportionately benefits.

Public expenditure per person in Northern Ireland is around 45% higher than in the Republic. The economist John FitzGerald calculates that even if Northern Ireland came debt-free (without taking its share of UK national debt), Southern funding of public services in the North would reduce Irish Gross National Income by 3% and could leave the Northern standard of living 20% above that in the South.

In simple terms, that would mean poorer Southerners being taxed to send money to better-off Northerners. That would be neither a recipe for social cohesion nor a model that would sustain Southern understanding of culturally painful measures to welcome in hundreds of thousands of people, many of whom would seem sullenly ungrateful.

Irish welfare benefits, for instance, are more generous – and Northern Ireland has a higher percentage of its population on benefits.

Yet while many pro-unity campaigners maximise Northern Ireland's economic problems, they then seek to minimise the cost of fixing those problems. The scale of the subvention is open to debate. Sinn Féin's optimistic analysis discounts a host of budget lines, including military and overseas spending – as well as making no provision for Northern Ireland being left with a portion of the UK national debt (the Irish Free State agreed to take a share of UK national debt in 1921, although this arrangement was soon abolished). Debt might be counterbalanced by a successful argument that Northern Ireland deserves a share of UK national assets – but if that's the case, almost any figure could be argued to be appropriate, depending on the criteria used.

Unequally divided wealth

National income per head, constant prices, index 1998=100

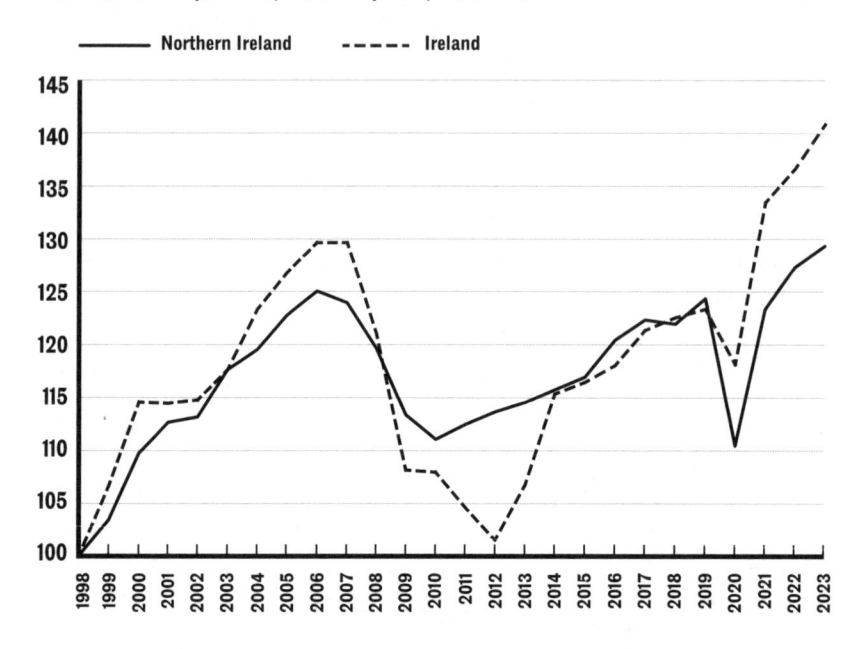

——— Northern Ireland   - - - - - Ireland

Real national income is shown here. For Ireland we used the modified gross national income (GNI*) at constant market prices per head and compared it with the GDP of Northern Ireland per head using 1998 as the base index as a starting point. Source: Office for National Statistics.

Sinn Féin says the final subvention figure will be determined by negotiation. In that, it is correct. This won't simply be a piece of accounting whose rules must be coldly applied. While there are some precedents, they are non-binding and open to significant interpretation. But Sinn Féin seems to assume that Ireland will secure remarkable gains from such a process. In truth, any negotiation involves give and take. In this negotiation, Ireland will be in an unavoidably weak position. It will be legally already committed to buying the car – but now arguing over the price of the car.

The more one examines this, the more uncertain the outcome could be. Much will come down to the whims of whoever happens to be in charge in London; if that's a nationalistic politician such as Nigel Farage, is it really likely that he'll just shrug as billions of pounds vanish?

A 2024 study led by FitzGerald and Morgenroth estimated that the initial cost of a united Ireland would be at least €8 billion per year, rising to as much as €20 billion per year. FitzGerald said the sums were so vast that for citizens of the Republic unity would result in 'an immediate, major reduction in their living standards'.[24]

Professor John Doyle disputed this, coming up with a radically smaller figure of €2.5 billion per year.[25] Part of Doyle's figures rested on public sector salaries in Northern Ireland not immediately being raised to provide equality with their Southern counterparts. But more significant still is the issue of pensions. Doyle – like Sinn Féin – believes the UK would have a moral obligation to pay state pensions to Northerners who'd paid National Insurance. But he concedes that there is no legal requirement for this.

The British state pension operates on a pay-as-you-go basis whereby National Insurance contributions today pay for pensions today, rather than individuals having a reserved pot of money. It would be grossly unfair (and here I must declare an interest) to those who've paid National Insurance to be told they will get no pension. But legally there would be nothing we could do about it. Realistically, the Irish state would have to pick up the bill if Britain were to refuse to pay, and that makes this economically significant for Southerners as well as Northerners.

The UK currently pays the pensions of Britons who retire to France or Spain. Where they reside is in one sense deemed irrelevant. The Scottish National Party used this to argue that it would be incongruous for Scots to be allowed to get their pension anywhere in the world except Scotland.

Yet while that argument seems superficially strong, the UK can do as it pleases. It could alter the terms of the pension (as it has done on issues such as the retirement age) at any point; in theory, it could scrap it completely, even if that would be politically impossible. The UK has also decided that some British nationals living abroad do not get annual pension increases – meaning a real-terms cut each year – so already that system distinguishes based on residency.

Whitehall could take the view that relatively modest numbers of expats are fundamentally distinct from an entire nation leaving, thus stopping all ongoing contributions to the fund from which pensions are paid. If Britain continued paying Northern Irish pensions, it would mean British taxpayers paying those in what might by then be a far wealthier state than Britain. Is it realistic that English taxpayers fund more generous pensions for the Northern Irish than for themselves when they leave the UK?

Of particular relevance to the Treasury in London will be the fear that, if Northern Ireland leaves the UK before Scotland, what happens in Northern Ireland will create a precedent for a much larger Scottish bill. Ultimately even the Scottish nationalists dropped the idea that Scotland wouldn't be liable for pensions.[26] Setting a precedent of generosity towards Northern Irish pensioners would make it easier for Scottish nationalists to win an independence referendum.

This will ultimately be the subject of negotiation, and that means uncertainty. David Eiser of the Fraser of Allander Institute has noted that 'there is no arbitration procedure for the break-up of a state, in which case the outcome will likely depend on which party has most to lose by a failure to agree'.[27]

If this was a messy breakup where the UK felt threatened by an Ireland likely to grow economically, it might not be incentivised to make things easy. And as recent Tory governments have demonstrated, there is no guarantee of an amenable administration in Downing Street that will play by unwritten rules of being nice. It would be dangerously complacent to believe that pensions will automatically be paid in perpetuity by a foreign nation.

Yet even accepting for the sake of argument that this would happen, there are other perils. UK pensions would continue to be paid in sterling but would have to be converted to euro. If Northern Ireland were to leave the Union, it would be likely to see sterling devalue, as happened after Brexit, with the markets taking this as evidence of continued British decline and perhaps even a portent of the full collapse of the Union. That would mean a real-terms pension cut for Northern Irish residents who, even if still paid the same sum in pounds, would find it bought fewer euros, which in turn bought less food or clothes.

If the UK were to break up entirely, with Scotland and perhaps even Wales leaving, would English taxpayers continue to supply billions of pounds for pensioners no longer part of their country?

The darkest possibility

The end of white rule in Rhodesia and South Africa demonstrated that dramatic transitions can be largely peaceful – but far more often such change is drenched in blood. The greatest risk of sustained serious violence right now is a botched attempt at Irish unity. Thoughtful observers have long appreciated this. John Whyte in 1990 warned against the traditional Marxist view that without Britain's support, Protestants were likely to accept unity rather than fight to create their own state.

Whyte, an erudite Irish historian and political scientist of moderate views, warned that this might 'underestimate the intensity of Protestant feelings ... they seem to go beyond what is warranted by the real differences in interest involved, and to have deep psychological roots. In such circumstances, people may show more intransigence than could be justified on a rational calculus of profit and loss.'[28]

This grasps the danger of simply assuming that because such violence would almost certainly fail, it won't happen. Those who threatened or carried out violence in 1912, 1916, the 1950s, the Troubles and at other points often had little reason to believe that they would militarily succeed. It didn't stop them, and many of those people are now venerated.

Even if it can be argued that a united Ireland would be unquestionably better, if there is a significant possibility that the journey towards that destination would involve bloodshed, it is a fundamentally different proposition. If it were possible to calculate now how many dead there might be, what figure would be acceptable? One? Twenty? A hundred?

Ideologues are comfortable with far higher figures; the most extreme are willing to kill or to die if it brings about unity or secures the Union. Most of us see this as grotesque, especially given how marginal the difference now is between Ireland and Britain, two advanced and wealthy western societies that respect the rule of law, treat minorities well and seek to look after their poorest residents. It is not irresponsible to raise the possibility of violence; it is irresponsible and indeed immoral to play this down in the hope that it won't happen.

Whyte observed that

> for civil war to break out, it is not necessary for a majority of inhabitants to desire it. Quite small numbers of extremists on each side can force a situation where, by reprisal and counter-reprisal, the peacefully inclined majority are obliged to seek protection from, and then give support to, the paramilitaries of their own community. This is how civil war began in the Lebanon in 1975.[29]

The most dangerous circumstances involve a narrow vote in favour of unity where there is a widely believed perception among unionists that the result was corrupted by vote-stealing or dirty money or other illegality. Donald Trump's ability, without any evidence, to convince tens of millions of Americans that a demonstrably fair election was rigged demonstrates how this can happen. Here, the danger is far greater because there is a long history of vote-stealing. As recently as 2017, the SDLP accused Sinn Féin of having stolen votes to win a Westminster seat. That was an allegation originating not from unionists but from within nationalism.

It should be possible to design a process – perhaps involving indelible ink on the hand of each voter and masses of independent observers – that will convince most reasonable people that it is fair. But as Trump's claims show, not everyone is reasonable.

Historically, mainstream unionism's willingness to endorse radical unconstitutional methods has risen as Britain's support has

The case against a united Ireland

been in question. Almost all of unionism views the original UVF as heroic defenders against their absorption into a hostile united Ireland. Yet the UVF imported thousands of rifles, threatened insurrection against His Majesty's forces, and used the threat of bloody civil war to secure partition. That is the memory that a section of unionism will recall if it believes – however absurdly – that a border poll has been rigged.

Countering this would require a credible armed alternative. Yet the Republic's Defence Forces are farcically ill-equipped for such a task. Perhaps that is one of the reasons that most Southerners intuitively fear that violence could accompany a united Ireland.[30]

At the time of writing, there are three Irish naval patrol vessels but only one can go to sea because of manpower shortages. Naval vessels have been going to sea without working guns.[31] Loyalist paramilitaries' membership is more than double that of the Irish army. There are no Irish fighter aircraft of any description. Angry loyalists aren't going to be sailing up the Liffey in warships or flying bombing sorties over Cork, but a state needs to have a monopoly on the use of force, which is democratically and legally controlled.

Guns entered Northern Ireland from Germany by sea in 1912. As an island nation, smuggling on small boats is an obvious possibility. Importation of weapons on small aircraft or by drone needs to be taken seriously.

That would mean massive expenditure on the Defence Forces to prepare for a scenario that might never materialise. Part of the reason why Ireland has so much disposable wealth is that it has outsourced the cost of defence to others. With limited prospect of invasion, it has been able to rely on the RAF (Royal Air Force) to police threats in Irish airspace and the Royal Navy or other NATO (North Atlantic Treaty Organization) forces to deal with any serious maritime threat.

Investing in native defence capabilities would mean massive investment over many years. Those who argue that Northern Ireland's enormous cash subsidy from London each year is less than it seems point to issues such as Northern Ireland's contribution to the UK's armed forces. That fails to grapple with the increased defence spending that would be necessary to avoid Ireland's military weakness leaving it wide open to attack.

By contrast, Northern Ireland benefits from defence provided by a standing army, navy and air force capable of responding to domestic and international threats, and is protected by UK cybersecurity capabilities, which are increasingly critical in a digital world.

I can live with unity or Union. Even if the economic claims turn out to be wrong, I can live with being poorer. But I don't want to live, and I don't want my children to live, with civil war or anything approaching it.

Yet even setting aside the darkest possibility, there is every reason to believe that at least some unionists will not come willingly into a nation of which they want no part. The writer Malachi O'Doherty considered what unionists might do if they want to be recalcitrant: they would demand recognition as a special ethnic group, they'd demand equality monitoring to prevent discrimination, they'd fly the Union flag or the Ulster banner from all public buildings in their territories, they would demand reserved places in public employment, they might change street names and railway station names to celebrate their heroes, they would resist any attempt to make the Irish language compulsory in schools, and there 'will be leverage around other issues that we cannot predict'. Where demands are resisted, he warned, they will grow, and if the state is heavy-handed in crushing such dissent, then it may spread to those previously uncommitted.[32]

But violence is not the only risk. Repeatedly, the Republic's electorate has shown itself to be rebellious when voting in referendums. Even where the entire political establishment urges it to vote one way, the population not infrequently does the opposite.

An under-appreciated peril of the Good Friday Agreement's requirement for a Southern referendum on unity is that the Southern electorate cannot be taken for granted; it could vote down what its leaders agree.

There is a consensus – founded on good evidence – that Southern voters would inevitably back a united Ireland, almost irrespective of what proposition is put to them. It remains very likely that they would, but this is fertile territory for complacency. Were Northern Ireland to vote for unity but the South to vote against it, that would be a gut-punch to Northern nationalists, but it would also be unexpectedly painful for unionists. If most of Northern Ireland's inhabitants no longer want it to exist, then their dream is over because Northern Ireland's long-term existence would be impossible with the majority of its inhabitants having voted against it – yet Northerners of all descriptions would find themselves unwanted even when they'd finally agreed to what, for more than a century, they'd been told by the South they should do.

An irreversible decision

In Northern Ireland, voting for Irish unity is more consequential than voting to retain the Union because it is irreversible. If you vote for the Union and the UK subsequently descends into anarchy, there's a life raft: the law compels the UK to hold a border poll if there's evidence a majority in Northern Ireland want a united Ireland.

But there is no credible prospect of the reverse being true: no matter how bad Irish unity might prove to be, the idea of Northern Ireland leaving to rejoin the UK is virtually impossible. That means that voting against the Union requires more certainty than voting for what is its temporary continuation, contingent on the views of Northern Ireland's inhabitants.

And the future is a necessarily uncertain place. Brexit has been a bungling national embarrassment for the UK. But that doesn't mean that the EU is without serious flaws. It contains democratic shortcomings that now constrain Irish sovereignty in a growing number of areas – including defence, where Irish neutrality is being strained to breaking.

As EU nations lurch rightwards, Irish isolationism will only go so far. For good or ill, it is locked into the EU and whatever the EU's dominant nations decide will have to be implemented.

The two states on this island are imperfect, but so is every other state in the history of humankind. Brexit has emphasised to many consumers the importance of the UK's economic union. What they once took for granted – free trade with Britain – has been disrupted by the Irish Sea border. If a supplier can't or won't sell a specialised product to Northern Ireland due to sea border bureaucracy, it might not be available in the Republic because that is a far smaller marketplace. In theory, the vastness of the entire EU marketplace is available; in practice – as anyone who's tried to buy something online from a French or German website knows – language barriers and product specifications often mean impenetrable complexity, even before increased postage is considered.

Irish unity would mean amplifying such disruption to an extraordinary extent. It is a stubborn fact that Northern Ireland is embedded within the UK economy in ways most of us have always taken for granted. The Irish Sea border has partially detached Northern Ireland from the British economy, but to fully sever that link would involve immense economic disruption that ordinary people would notice.

Beyond economics, there is a contradiction in how republicans in the South denounce the Republic as almost a failed state while in the North presenting the Republic as a beacon of what Northern Ireland could be. The reality is that while Northern Ireland has deep problems, so does the Republic. Corruption in public life is acceptable to an alarming degree. This isn't just about Charlie Haughey or brown envelopes to politicians decades ago. In the 2024 Irish general election, Michael Lowry, described by an official tribunal as behaving in a way that was 'profoundly corrupt to a degree that was nothing short of breathtaking', was not only comfortably re-elected, but was kingmaker in deciding whether the current Irish government got to govern.[33] Gerry Hutch, openly known as a top gangster, received more than 3,000 votes, only narrowly missing out on a seat.

Being small allows for nimble Irish movement to take advantage of economic niches. But it also involves peril. When a great recessionary wave comes, the small are especially vulnerable. Booms are bigger, but so are busts. While being in the EU is something of a bulwark, Ireland's experience of the punishing terms extracted by the EU in 2010 illustrate how other European capitals will prioritise themselves in extremis.

Greater efficiencies talked of by unity advocates mean cuts to public sector jobs in Northern Ireland. They're right that this would in many cases be more efficient – but that means lost jobs. About one in three Northern Irish workers are in the public sector. This is too high; nevertheless, it is a fact.[34] A united Ireland would mean either cutting many of those jobs, or Southerners paying much of their wages – and those wages would have to rise sharply to match their Southern counterparts if there was to be pay equality. The financial writer Paul Gosling is among the few advocates of unity to be straight with the public about this, proposing a reduction in the size of Northern Ireland's public sector to that of the Republic.[35] Gosling says that could mean saving about £1.7 billion per year.[36]

To paraphrase Huey Long, the 1930s governor of Louisiana, in a united Ireland the people of Northern Ireland might get good government – and some of them aren't going to like it.

Keeping Northern Ireland's worst bits

The only feasible form of unity right now is a continuation of Northern Ireland on a devolved basis. Essentially the Agreement would continue but be inverted: devolution would endure with the cheque Stormont spends coming from Dublin rather than London; rather than sending MPs to Westminster Northern Ireland would send TDs to the Dáil; and much of what makes Northern Ireland what it is – the Northern Ireland Civil Service, the Northern Ireland football team, the PSNI – could endure.

At first glance, this is a far more attractive proposition for unionists than a unitary state ruled from Dublin. They would no longer be part of the UK, but they'd still have Northern Ireland, the state their ancestors had built and they'd come to love.

But this would almost certainly be a mirage. It would mean keeping most of the bad bits of Northern Ireland while losing its key benefit – being part of a much larger UK. Devolution has been shambolic. It has failed to provide basic good government and has seen parties forcefully shackled together while presiding over the decay of public services. This is unsustainable, whether in the Union or in an all-island state.

Power-sharing rules mean that Sinn Féin would have a veto power that could pull down devolution and keep it down. If it did so, the only credible alternative would be direct rule from Dublin. Thus, whatever promises anyone made, one party would retain the sole power to force rule from Dublin. Even if not using this power, its threat would give the party disproportionate control whenever there was a row in the Executive.

Polling shows decidedly hostile Southern attitudes to changing their state in order to accommodate Northerners. Most Southerners oppose a new flag, oppose a new anthem, oppose paying more tax for unity, oppose rejoining the Commonwealth, oppose giving unionists a guaranteed number of cabinet seats, and oppose retaining Stormont.

Much of this is likely founded as much in ignorance of what unity would really mean as in nostalgic patriotism. Even among those who on paper are most committed, there are other pressing concerns. Only 36% of Southern Sinn Féin supporters said in 2021 that a united Ireland is 'very important'.[37]

Abandoning a precious health system

For Northerners, the practical benefits of the Union are best encapsulated in the NHS. The principle that underpins this system, of healthcare free to everyone regardless of wealth or status, is precious. The NHS arose from one of the most benevolently egalitarian decisions taken by any government in human history. Plenty of Southerners look with envy to this aspect of the British system.

The case against a united Ireland

In recent years, the NHS has had undeniably serious problems. Yet most people's experience of the NHS is very different. For a vast number of people, it's still a system that delivers their children, treats them when they are sick, and cares for them until their final breath. Eight out of ten people who use the health and social care services in Northern Ireland say they are happy with their experience.[38]

Flaws in the NHS can be fixed, even if that necessitates unpopular measures such as closing some smaller hospitals to centralise experts in centres of excellence. There are good political reasons to believe the NHS will not be abandoned politically: nothing unites the British public like its love for the NHS.

To abandon rather than work to fix this system would mean casting aside one of the great social achievements of the last century and replacing it with a system where money plays a far more prominent role. This isn't just about having to pay to see your doctor; that's just the most obvious aspect of a system where the profit motive is far more pronounced than in the NHS.

The NHS is just one of a multitude of great national organisations, many of them built over centuries, that Northern Ireland's inhabitants take for granted because they've always been there.

What Northern Ireland would lose

For all the flaws of the two states on this island, there is much about them that many people would miss. Northern Ireland's education system has historically been well regarded. It has now been overtaken by the Republic's, but this has been recognised rather than denied, with education minister Paul Givan instigating a radical programme of reform. Despite its problems, Northern Ireland's school system offers extraordinary choice, all funded by government – state, Catholic, Irish-medium and integrated schools. State-funded top-end grammars provide the sort of education that would otherwise cost thousands of pounds in private school fees. St Columba's College in Dublin charges €10,258 per pupil per year; Methodist College Belfast charges £140.[39]

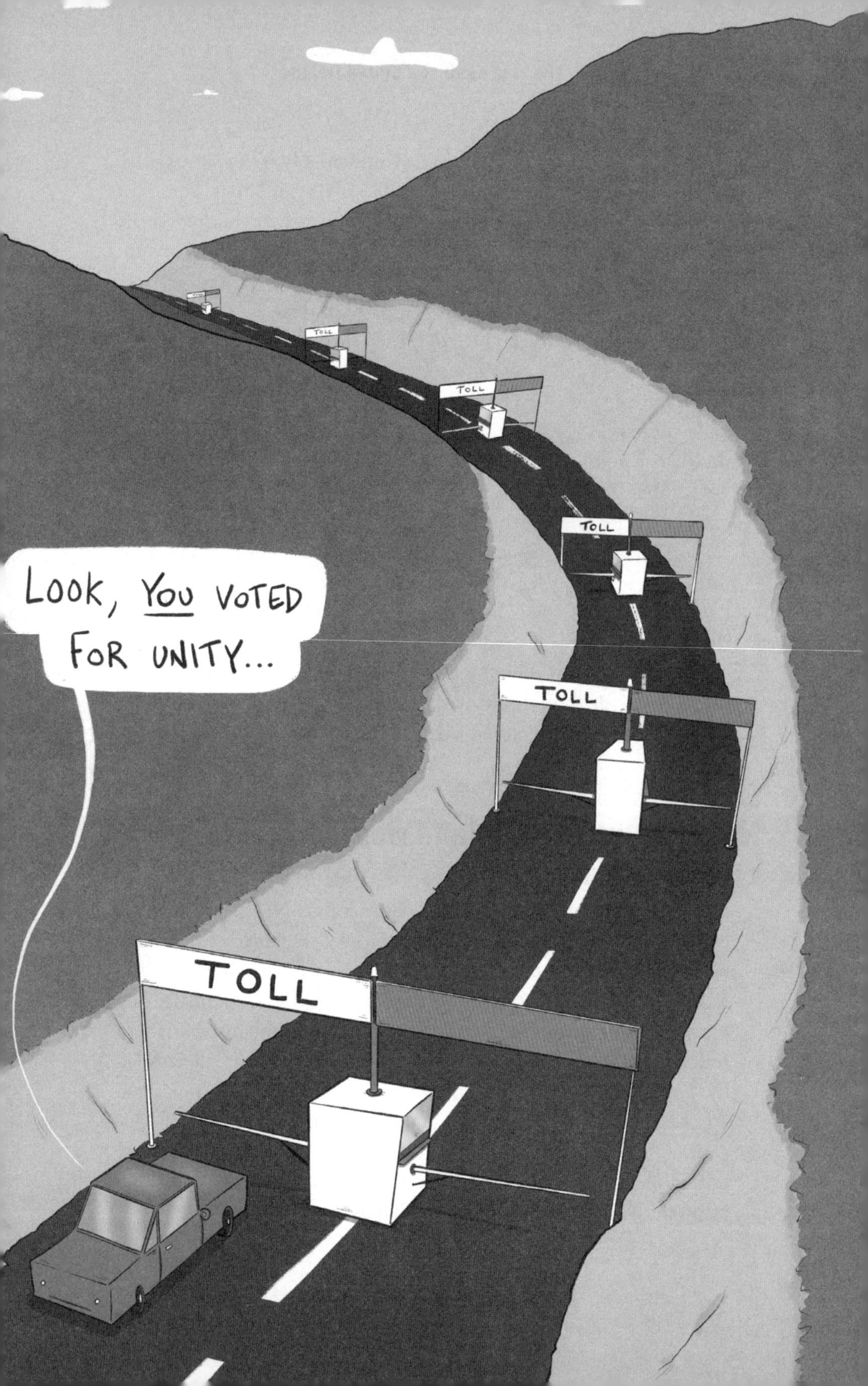
LOOK, YOU VOTED FOR UNITY...
TOLL
TOLL
TOLL
TOLL
TOLL

The case against a united Ireland

There are no toll roads in Northern Ireland, but travelling from Belfast to Cork and back would cost €19 in tolls.[40]

It is also naive to believe that the astronomical Southern investment necessary in Northern Ireland after unity could happen without pain that goes beyond the merely financial. The growth of a Belfast–Dublin–Cork corridor could see the west of the island left even further behind.

Likewise, even when rich the Republic has significant regional inequality. If regions like Donegal haven't been dragged up by Dublin's wealth, there is no guarantee that much of Northern Ireland would be, even if Belfast was.

Leaving the UK would mean losing the BBC, one of the world's great broadcasters. Its output – not just in news, but in culture, drama, music and stimulating national thinking – has been of incalculable benefit. The easy routines of *Question Time*, *Match of the Day*, Radio 1 *Breakfast*, or whatever it might be for each citizen according to their tastes, would be gone.[41] Even if they paid to subscribe to the BBC from outside the UK, it would not only be an extra expense, but it would be like tuning into American networks. For unionists, this would no longer be their country; what the politicians did in London would no longer be about decisions impacting their lives any more than would the day-to-day worries of the Bundestag.

The BBC is a superior broadcaster to RTÉ. That is not to denigrate the Irish national broadcaster any more than it is to say *The Times* is a better newspaper than the *Belfast Telegraph*, for which I write – the size of its audience means far more income, which can pay for more journalists, better production teams, more money to spend on drama, and so on.

RTÉ might incorporate BBC NI's former staff into its operation, but it's never going to be able to match the volume or the quality of the national and international output.

Leaving the UK would also mean the loss of a network of expertise that even a larger united Ireland would never be able to fully replicate. Take the Met Office, for instance – a crucial resource in forecasting not only tomorrow's weather, but climatic conditions decades hence. The Met Office has 2,200 employees; Met Éireann has about 10% of that number.[42]

The UK has powerful national conservation organisations such as the Royal Society for the Protection of Birds, the National Trust and the Woodland Trust, which are able to influence national policy through research funded by drawing on a far larger population.

In specialism after specialism, there are unalterable realities about being part of a country with about 10% of the UK population. The UK is a member of the UN Security Council, the G7 (Group of Seven) and the Commonwealth. It is the world's sixth-biggest economy; even after the economic mess of Brexit and the Irish boom, Ireland is 19 places behind.[43]

Border benefits

Often the border is viewed solely in negative terms, with no recognition of its benefits. Yet having part of our shared island homeland in the UK means that Britain – which will always be our huge next-door neighbour – has more strategic interest in the well-being of Ireland than in a wholly foreign country.

Without Northern Ireland in the UK, there is no guarantee that the Common Travel Area – which for now is a practical necessity – would continue. Post-unity, Britain could tighten immigration controls at our expense.

The Northern Ireland Protocol means uniquely unfettered access to both EU and UK markets. While not without downsides, if this leads to Northern Ireland prospering, as is at least theoretically possible, then voting for a united Ireland would almost certainly mean abandoning it.

For Northerners, while wages are lower, the single greatest expense for most people – housing – is dramatically cheaper, as are property taxes. With a massive public sector, mostly paid at UK-wide rates, this means that many workers are significantly better off than their counterparts across the rest of the UK.

The case against a united Ireland

The Covid-19 pandemic opened a new way in which the border can – entirely legally – be exploited to mutual advantage. It is now possible to have a Dublin job paid at high Dublin rates but live in Newry, Portadown or even Belfast, taking ever-improving trains once or twice a week to the office and working the rest of the time from a house that might cost half as much as those lived in by colleagues.

Good neighbourliness – to which the absence of violence is critical – can allow such pragmatic arrangements to flourish, to mutual benefit. The border can be a practical pain, but it can also be of practical benefit.

Conversely, even under the most benign circumstances imaginable, there would be incredible practical disruption in removing the border. Companies registered with the UK Companies House would have to re-register with the Irish Companies Registration Office and operate under different regulatory requirements.

The Post Office would be replaced by An Post. Royal Mail's legal obligation to deliver letters throughout the UK would no longer include Northern Ireland. An Post charges as much to send a letter to Britain as it does to South America – a second-class stamp that now costs 85p would suddenly cost €2.20. The significance of online shopping means this would be more problematic in reverse; Northern Ireland benefits from parcel delivery that is generally set at UK rates – delivering a UK parcel to Northern Ireland is currently about half the cost of sending it to the Republic.

If unity meant a unitary state, specialists within the UK system – such as lawyers with expert knowledge of UK case law – would find such niche knowledge of little benefit in a new system.

At the simplest level, individual citizens would find that many of the public bodies they know would likely change, making it more difficult to work out how to get things done.

Northern Ireland has an unemployment rate half that of the Republic's and a globally significant cybersecurity centre, helped by being plugged into Government Communications Headquarters (GCHQ) and the wider UK national security apparatus.

YEH, I'M MAKING FIVE TIMES WHAT I'D MAKE UP NORTH. SOME DAY, I'LL BE ABLE TO AFFORD A WINDOW
WELCOME

The case against a united Ireland

It has a far more generous legal holiday entitlement than the Republic – 28 days to the South's 20. It benefits from London being one of the world's main financial centres, both through the enormous subsidy that pays for public services and through spill-over employment as London firms utilise cheaper labour in Belfast for back-office functions.

The cost of living in Belfast is 30% less than in Dublin, according to Numbeo, a price comparison website; rents are 52% lower, a monthly train ticket is 34% cheaper, a beer is 26% cheaper – even a McDonald's is 24% cheaper.[44] Research by the Economic and Social Research Institute in January 2025 found that families on low incomes in the Republic find it harder to convert their income into an adequate standard of living than those in Northern Ireland.[45]

Patrick Honohan, former governor of the Central Bank of Ireland, said in 2021: 'Ireland is a prosperous country, but not as prosperous as is often thought because of the inappropriate use of misleading, albeit conventional statistics.'[46]

If Northern benefits and public sector salaries were to be increased, it would lead to dramatic inflation that would disadvantage those on lower incomes, particularly pensioners receiving a fixed pension but seeing prices rise all around them, driven by the influx of Southern money.

The position of Sinn Féin – the island's biggest party – on most of the key issues is that it has no position. Conveniently, it washes its hands of difficult choices by saying they should be considered by some future citizens' assembly. That's politically clever, but it means that the party can give no credible guarantees to anyone. If it doesn't know what sort of unity it wants to see, it can't reassure the people most wary of a party that to this day defends the slaughter of the innocent as collateral damage in republicanism's long war to secure Irish freedom.

Sam McBride

An epoch-defining choice

Uniquely perhaps among all the generations that have inhabited this isle, we hold something both precious and fragile. Risking it in the hope of something better could be an era-defining mistake. As the writer of Ecclesiastes observed, a living dog is better than a dead lion.

Whatever our aspirations, for now we should be able to unite around making both parts of the island work, making the two parts of the island understand each other better, and leaving it to the wisdom of our descendants at some long-distant juncture to decide if a near-invisible border should be removed.

Like the end of the world, the border's death has been long foretold. But just as the world has defied false prophets, so those who routinely show up for the Union's funeral find the corpse to be defiantly alive.

It has survived the loss of most of Ireland, an existential world war, the loss of empire, devolution, crises in the monarchy, sweeping social change, ethnic diversity, religious pluralism and Brexit. It has survived because it has worked. It endures because England, Scotland, Wales and Northern Ireland have separately decided for themselves that their future is better together than apart. It allows each of its constituent parts to be fully English, Scottish, Welsh, Northern Irish (or Irish) while being equally British. It is akin to the way in which footballers can line out against each other for their clubs, then come together for their country. Not everything in life is entirely binary.

The history of the Union is one of constant structural reform, much of it for the better. If history is a guide, the limits of its future evolution are beyond what we can now imagine.

Likewise, the Republic has defied those who scoffed at the idea that the Irish were capable of self-government. Its bureaucracy humiliated Britain in the Brexit negotiations and has presided over staggering economic growth and social change. This is not a failed island, but a flourishing one. The border isn't holding us back; removing it could be an act of hubristic downfall.

Postscript

The readiness is all (*Hamlet*, Act 5, Scene 2)

History often comes out of the blue. The world we inhabit is shaped by shocks. The Soviet Union collapsed very quickly and new states had to emerge – sometimes violently – from its ruins. German reunification came suddenly. The great banking crash of 2008 was one in which apparently obscure financial glitches became, with dizzying speed, a global crisis. Brexit was not really taken seriously as a live possibility until it was about to happen. Donald Trump's decision to prioritise America's relationship with Russia over its long-established alliance with western Europe flabbergasted most European Union governments, and his declaration of a trade war against pretty much everybody spread panic through the global economy. Closer to home, very few people in 1967 imagined that Northern Ireland was about to implode in a 30-year conflict.

But there is nothing shocking about the possibility of Irish unification. It has been fully and formally accepted as a legitimate and achievable goal at least since the Belfast Agreement of 1998. It is not inevitable but it is eminently foreseeable. This is an opportunity for which we should be grateful and of which we should take full advantage. Irish people will, at some point, face a momentous choice. But that moment should not come out of the blue. It is one that can be prepared for in such a way as to make the choice real and concrete. People on both sides of the border should be able to vote with their eyes open.

There is no reason to believe that a border poll is imminent, nor would it be wise to hold a referendum for a considerable period because even nationalist politicians are for now mostly only engaging with the issue rhetorically. The folly of the UK embarking on Brexit based on an ill-defined aspiration would be amplified exponentially in a decision of even greater magnitude taken in circumstances that are far more combustible.

A border poll can be held and – as two of the chapters of this book set out – Irish unity could work to create a settled, pluralist and prosperous island that is moving decisively beyond the bloody enmity of the past. That would require years of hard slog before a referendum and decades of difficult and for the most part terribly dull work after a vote for unity. It would also be infused with the energy of hope, encompassing both the fulfilment of centuries-old romantic dreams and the practical potential to fix systemic problems that have held back regions or groups of people on this island.

Demanding a sudden border poll without having done the work to prepare for one is not only infantile, but dangerous. Irish unity is a serious idea, and it deserves to be taken seriously. Those who want it to happen have to go beyond ritual recitations of demands either for a plebiscite or for someone else to do the planning for one. They have to assume that citizens are intelligent enough to understand that all big changes have downsides as well as upsides and have a right to an honest and well-grounded assessment of the balance between them.

For their part, unionists have failed overwhelmingly to engage with the task of persuading their neighbours to keep Northern Ireland within the Union. There are perfectly credible and logical arguments that they could make; their leaders just rarely prioritise such arguments over tribal squabbles or eye-poking.

Postscript

Some of this reluctance to engage may be rooted in a belief that preparing the ground for a border poll is simply opening the way to Irish unity. But it isn't – for two good reasons. First, much of what can be done to make a referendum meaningful – for example, sharing resources to create better health services on both sides of the border or boosting investment in public transport, education and green infrastructure – is well worth doing anyway. It makes life better for everyone, regardless of whether Northern Ireland ultimately opts to remain in the UK or join a united Ireland.

Second, before we get to 'yes' or 'no', there is 'maybe'. A border poll, especially in the North, will not be decided by those who already know how they will vote. Its outcome will be determined by the growing number of people who are open to persuasion. The open-minded will not be swayed by slogans or appeals to tribal solidarity. They will want good answers to hard questions. Both sides will have to be prepared to make arguments grounded on facts about the present and realistic projections about the future.

We should bear in mind that by the time border polls are held, it is very likely that an even greater number of voters will be people whose personal and family histories lie very far from the worlds of either Irish nationalism or Irish unionism. Already around 10% of those living in Northern Ireland were born outside the UK and 20% of those living in the Republic were born outside Ireland. Very many of those who go to the polls will have identities that do not align themselves with traditional Green/Orange, Protestant/Catholic or British/Irish binaries. They will be looking not for historic vindication or vengeance, but for better futures for themselves and their children.

It is easy for unionism and nationalism to dismiss each other's vision as ludicrous. Each has inherited its own history of lazy stereotypes: unionists caricaturing the Republic as parochial, backward and priest-ridden; nationalists seeing Britain – and Britishness – as the root of most of Ireland's woes and presenting unity as the simplistic solution. Yet both sides have strong and wholly respectable reasons to believe that life would be better under their constitutional preference. Both constitutional visions entail reasonable propositions, not absurd fantasies.

The modern UK and Ireland are not the places of the 1600s or the 1920s or even the 1980s. They are among the most sophisticated, most equal, most prosperous, most democratic, most stable and least repressive societies the world has ever seen. There are billions of people in the world who would love to have the opportunity to be part of either the UK or Ireland. We do not sufficiently cherish the blessing of a choice between what are, in global and historical terms, two outstanding options. This is akin to the choice between being part of the US or Canada, not whether to be part of Ukraine or Russia.

That was not always so. It wasn't true for a Protestant in Monaghan in 1912; it wasn't true for a Catholic in west Belfast in 1950. There were legitimate fears for both unionists and nationalists at the time of partition and for most of the decades since. But too many people believe we are still, to a significant extent, in that place. We need to recognise that the terrain on both sides of the border has shifted, in some respects beyond recognition.

For many people, of course, rational arguments will be irrelevant. Even if one option or the other could be objectively proved to be superior, it wouldn't alter how they'd vote because they feel a keen sense of identity with either Britain or Ireland. This is wholly legitimate, and doesn't have to be viewed as backward or sectarian. We all feel affinity to certain collective ideals, whether religious or secular, and in many societies national identity is a healthy unifying force.

Yet even those whose vote would primarily be an expression of identity should think carefully about their decision. Considering the arguments might not alter their vote in any way – but they'll be stuck with the consequences and so should be forewarned of what might lie ahead. And they all have an interest in the result of the poll achieving as wide an acceptance as possible – a condition that is much more likely to exist if the referendum campaigns are conducted rationally and respectfully and if genuine anxieties are addressed with credible reassurances.

Postscript

When the tribal allegiances are stripped away – or don't exist because a voter has come to this island from abroad – this question largely comes down to an individual's appetite for risk. For the risk-averse, there are compelling arguments to hold on to the status quo. That doesn't mean that sticking with what we've come to know is risk-free. It's not, any more than the UK staying in the EU would have been risk-free. No nation or union stands still; changes over time might make what now is tolerable at some point intolerable.

But even there the risk tilts in favour of the status quo: if a united Ireland is rejected in a first border poll, that's not the end of the matter. It can return in a second – or third or fourth, or however many we want – referendum seven years later. By contrast, a vote for Irish unity will be final.

Central to the holding of a border poll in a responsible manner will be basic cross-border education. A great many people on either side of the border are genuinely ignorant of even basic elements of what this question would involve. A surprisingly large percentage of the population has never even crossed the border.

As author and mediator Padraig O'Malley says of Southerners' desire for unity: 'The aspiration is strong, but the commitment is weak; sentiment is frequently contradictory, the result of southerners not having to give much thought to the matter.'[1] Properly addressing Southern lack of knowledge of the North and Northern ignorance of the South would take many years. It's far more than simply producing a document or a series of government-organised events.

Much of the talk of the supposed inevitability of a united Ireland rests on sagging pillars. Brexit was going to blow apart the Union, convincing unionists that they'd be better off joining the Republic in the EU. Yet the polls have shown minimal movement in Northern unionists' allegiance to Britain. Then Scotland was going to leave the UK, with its first minister, Nicola Sturgeon, hailed as one of the stateswomen of the age. Instead, her leadership collapsed amid scandal and her nationalist party has lost ground. Then a succession of hapless and disreputable Conservative governments were going to drive the Union apart. Instead, the Tories have been electorally crushed and a boringly centrist Labour prime minister is in Downing Street.

Then Sinn Féin's emergence as Northern Ireland's largest party and its 'inevitable' emergence as the biggest party in the Dáil was going to be constitutionally transformative. Instead, the party's progress in the South has stalled and it has settled down into pragmatic governance with the DUP in the North.

Many of these claims stemmed from historical ignorance. It's true that history doesn't guarantee the future; but the fact that the Union has for hundreds of years muddled through bigger crises than these points to powerful institutional, cultural and economic forces that are not easily dislodged. This British 'endism' about the Union, as the academic Arthur Aughey calls it, is not new.

Yet it is also true that unionism has repeatedly failed to adapt to the radical changes that have happened all around it. Where it has come to accept reality, it has almost always done so reluctantly and after futile but rhetorically ferocious resistance. A large number of unionists still aspire to 'unionist unity', which at its crudest involves a nostalgic attempt to recreate the flawed party that for the first half-century of partition managed to build a state that was viable in the short term but was antithetical to the sagacious strategic advice of Lord Carson, who at the founding of Northern Ireland told unionism 'Let them see that the Catholic minority have nothing to fear from a Protestant majority.'[2]

The only certainty is that change – climatic, demographic, cultural, social, economic and political – will continue, both on the island of Ireland and in the international contexts that shape its destiny. The ultimate question in relation to unity will be whether, in a turbulent world, more people prefer the comforts of the familiar or believe that the challenges of the future can best be met in a transformed Ireland. While much of what will happen in the meantime is currently hard to imagine, this is one choice that we can control. We have been given the benefits of peace and time in which to consider this decision carefully. History tends to be sparing with those gifts.

Endnotes

Introduction

[1] The ARINS research is available at: https://www.ria.ie/research-programmes/arins/.

Chapter 1

[1] *Hansard*, vol. 33, 10 December 1982, c. 1138.
[2] 'Britain's snap election further opportunity united Ireland – Sinn Féin', *Anglo-Celt*, 18 April 2017.
[3] 'Letter from Seán MacBride to Ernest Bevin (London)', 9 March 1949, *Documents on Irish Foreign Policy*, available at: https://www.difp.ie/volume-9/1949/irelands-reasons-for-not-joining-nato/4891/ (22 April 2025).
[4] Arthur Griffith, *The resurrection of Hungary* (Dublin, 1904), 79.
[5] 'Letter from Frederick H. Boland to Seán Murphy (Paris)', 7 February 1949, *Documents on Irish Foreign Policy*, available at: https://www.difp.ie/volume-9/1949/irelands-reply-to-american-invitation-to-ireland-to-join-the-atlantic-pact/4856/ (22 April 2025). See also Dáil Éireann debates, 6 March 1958, 17 April 1956, 22 April 1936 and 27 June 2016, available at: https://www.oireachtas.ie/en/debates/ (22 April 2025).
[6] Quoted in Robert Lynch, *The partition of Ireland 1918–1925* (Cambridge, 2019), 113–37: 120.
[7] *Irish Times*, 21 December 1919.
[8] Quoted in Lynch, *The partition of Ireland*, 113–37: 119.
[9] Colin Harvey, 'Let "the people" decide: reflections on constitutional change and "concurrent consent"', *Irish Studies in International Affairs* 32 (2) (2021), 382–405: 388.
[10] Quoted in Christoper McCrudden, Oran Doyle and David Kenny, 'The franchise in Irish unification referendums', *Irish Studies in International Affairs* 32 (2) (2021), 182–213: 182.
[11] Oran Doyle, 'Populist constitutionalism and constituent power', *German Law Journal* 20 (special issue 2) (2019), 161–80: 175.
[12] Gerard Hogan, *The origins of the Irish constitution 1928–1941* (Dublin, 2012), 210–12.
[13] Basil Brooke, 'Ulster's best interests lie with the United Kingdom' in Northern Ireland Government, *Why the border must be: the Northern Ireland case in brief*, available at: https://cain.ulster.ac.uk/othelem/docs/nigov56.htm (24 July 2025).
[14] The Sunningdale Agreement (December 1973) available at: https://cain.ulster.ac.uk/events/sunningdale/agreement.htm (22 April 2025).
[15] The Supreme Court, 'R (on the application of Miller and another) (Respondents) v Secretary of State for Exiting the European Union (Appellant)', 8 November 2016, available at: https://www.supremecourt.uk/cases/uksc-2016-0196.html (22 April 2025).

[16] Jennifer Todd, Joanne McEvoy and John Doyle, 'Time for deliberation, not decision, on the shape of a new united Ireland: evidence from the ARINS survey focus groups', *Irish Studies in International Affairs* 34 (2) (2023), 122–48: 130.

[17] Brendan O'Leary and John Garry, 'Health service, economy and peace are key concerns about united Ireland', *Irish Times*, 5 December 2022.

[18] Independent Reporting Commission, Sixth Report, 5 December 2023, available at: https://www.ircommission.org/news/irc-sixth-report-published-5-december-2023 (22 April 2025).

[19] Damian Loscher, 'Irish Times/ARINS poll: support for United Ireland is strong, but debate on costs and compromises to come first', *Irish Times*, 2 December 2023.

[20] BBC, 'Plymouth shooting: who can own a firearm or shotgun in the UK?', 24 August 2021, available at: https://www.bbc.com/news/uk-58198857 (22 April 2025).

[21] Kathryn Torney, 'Who owns Northern Ireland's 153,000 legally held guns?', *The Detail*, 23 August 2012, available at: https://www.thedetail.tv/articles/who-owns-northern-ireland-s-153-000-legally-held-guns (22 April 2025).

[22] John Garry, Brendan O'Leary, Paul Gillespie and Roland Gjoni, 'Public attitudes to Irish unification: evidence on models and process from a deliberative forum in Ireland', *Irish Studies in International Affairs* 33 (2) (2022).

[23] Údarás na Gaeltachta, 'New research shows strong position of Irish language in Ireland's identity', 6 November 2024, available at: https://udaras.ie/en/news/new-research-shows-strong-position-of-irish-language-in-irelands-identity/ (22 April 2025).

[24] Pat Leahy, 'Little interaction between people living North and South, new polls show', *Irish Times*, 28 January 2023.

[25] Brendan O'Leary and John Garry, 'Integrated vs devolved: two possible forms for united Ireland that divide opinion North and South', *Irish Times*, 10 December 2022.

[26] Garry et al., 'Public attitudes to Irish unification'.

[27] The Nobel Prize, 'John Hume interview', 31 August 2006, available at: https://www.nobelprize.org/prizes/peace/1998/hume/interview/ (22 April 2025).

[28] John Garry and Brendan O'Leary, 'Debate over symbols of a united Ireland shows up a big North–South difference', *Irish Times*, 5 December 2022.

[29] John Garry, Brendan O'Leary and Jamie Pow, 'Can the Red Hand of Ulster be transformed into a unifying image for the island of Ireland?', *Irish Times*, 22 January 2024.

[30] *The Belfast Agreement: an agreement reached at the multi-party talks on Northern Ireland*, 10 April 1998, 28, available at: https://www.gov.uk/government/publications/the-belfast-agreement (22 April 2025) (emphasis added).

[31] John FitzGerald and Edgar Morgenroth, 'Northern Ireland subvention: possible unification effects', *IIEA*, 4 April 2024, available at: iiea.com/publications/northern-ireland-subvention-possible-unification-effects (21 April 2025). Esmond Birnie, 'The subvention matters: a response to "Why the 'subvention' does not matter: Northern Ireland and the all-Ireland economy" by John Doyle', *Irish Studies in International Affairs* 34 (2) (2023), 359–94.

[32] Oireachtas Joint Committee on the Implementation of the Good Friday Agreement debate, 2 May 2024.

[33] FitzGerald and Morgenroth, 'Northern Ireland subvention'.

[34] Fionnán Sheehan, 'Majority favour a united Ireland, but just 22pc would pay for it', *Irish Independent*, 1 May 2021.

Endnotes

[35] Red C/*Business Post*, 'Opinion poll report November 2021', available at: https://redcresearch.com/wp-content/uploads/2021/11/Business-Post-RED-C-Opinion-Poll-Report-Nov-2021-.pdf (21 July 2025).

[36] 'UK debt and the Scotland independence referendum', available at: https://assets.publishing.service.gov.uk/media/5a7c8633e5274a2674eab3f5/uk_debt_and_the_Scotland_independence_referendum.pdf (21 July 2025).

[37] FitzGerald and Morgenroth, 'Northern Ireland subvention'.

[38] Karina Doorley, Michele Gubello and Dora Tuda, *Drivers of income inequality in Ireland and Northern Ireland*, ESRI Research Series 196 (Dublin, 2004).

[39] Ciara Fitzpatrick and Charles O'Sullivan, 'Comparing social security provision North and South of Ireland: past developments and future challenges', *Irish Studies in International Affairs* 32 (2) (2021), 283–313.

[40] O'Leary and Garry, 'Health service, economy and peace are key concerns about united Ireland'.

[41] Todd et al., 'Time for deliberation, not decision, on the shape of a new united Ireland', 130.

[42] BMA, 'NHS under pressure – Northern Ireland', 11 July 2024, available at: https://www.bma.org.uk/advice-and-support/nhs-delivery-and-workforce/pressures/nhs-under-pressure-northern-ireland (22 April 2025).

[43] Department of Health, 'Life expectancy in Northern Ireland 2020–22', 6 December 2023, available at: https://www.health-ni.gov.uk/news/life-expectancy-northern-ireland-2020-22 (22 April 2025); CSO, 'Measuring Ireland's progress 2022', 23 February 2024, available at: https://www.cso.ie/en/releasesandpublications/ep/p-mip/measuringirelandsprogress2022/keyfindings/ (22 April 2025).

[44] O'Leary and Garry, 'Health service, economy and peace are key concerns about united Ireland'.

[45] Ireland's Future, 'An opportunity for a world class, all island national health service', n.d., available at: https://irelandsfuture.com/wp-content/uploads/2023/05/IF-An-Opportunity-for-a-World-Class-All-Island-National-Health-Service-An-Irish-National-Health-Service-1.pdf (22 April 2025).

[46] Sinn Féin, 'A national health service for a united Ireland', n.d., available at: https://www.sinnfein.ie/files/2018/United_Ireland_Health.pdf (22 April 2025).

[47] Deirdre Heenan, 'Cross-border cooperation health in Ireland', *Irish Studies in International Affairs* 32 (2) (2021), 117–36.

[48] Anne Matthews, 'A crowded stage: a response to "Cross-border cooperation health in Ireland" by Deirdre Heenan', *Irish Studies in International Affairs* 32 (2) (2021), 137–41: 137.

[49] Dáil Éireann Parliamentary Question 197, 23 October 2024, available at: https://www.oireachtas.ie/en/debates/question/2024-10-23/197/#pq_197 (22 April 2025).

[50] Oireachtas Joint Committee on Health debate, 26 October 2022, available at: https://www.oireachtas.ie/en/debates/debate/joint_committee_on_health/2022-10-26/3/ (22 April 2025).

[51] Adele Bergin and Seamus McGuinness, *Modelling productivity levels in Ireland and Northern Ireland*, ESRI Research Series 152 (Dublin, 2022), v.

[52] Bergin and McGuinness, *Modelling productivity levels in Ireland and Northern Ireland*; Adele Bergin and Seamus McGuinness, 'Who is better off? Measuring

cross-border differences in living standards, opportunities and quality of life on the island of Ireland', *Irish Studies in International Affairs* 32 (2) 2021, 143–60: 152.

[53] Vani K. Borooah and Colin Knox, 'Inequality, segregation and poor performance: the education system in Northern Ireland', *Educational Review* 69 (3) (2016), 318–36.

[54] HEPI, 'New reports shed light on differences in higher education fees and funding systems across the UK', 6 February 2024, available at: https://www.hepi.ac.uk/2024/02/06/new-reports-shed-light-on-differences-in-higher-education-fees-and-funding-systems-across-the-uk/ (22 April 2025).

[55] Pivotal, 'Retaining and regaining talent in Northern Ireland', 24 March 2021, available at: https://www.pivotalpolicy.org/our-work/news-events/2021/03/retaining-and-regaining-talent (22 April 2025).

[56] Queen's University Belfast, 'Vice-chancellor urges NI Executive to invest in young people to reap long-term economic benefits', 7 February 2024, available at: https://www.qub.ac.uk/News/Allnews/2024/Vice-ChancellorurgesNIExecutivetoinvestinyoungpeopletoreaplong-termeconomicbenefits.html (22 April 2025).

[57] Pivotal, 'Retaining and regaining talent in Northern Ireland'.

[58] *Department of Education Statistical Bulletin*, 2024, available at: https://assets.gov.ie/302847/680bf2d0-b00f-4139-853f-246e198e706d.pdf (2 May 2025).

[59] Carl O'Brien, 'Churches are half-empty. So why does the Catholic Church still control so many of our primary schools?', *Irish Times*, 14 September 2024.

[60] Jennifer Todd, 'Unionism, identity and Irish unity: paradigms, problems and paradoxes', *Irish Studies in International Affairs* 32 (2) (2021), 53–77: 66.

[61] Carl O'Brien, 'Prof Hugh Brady: "Quality of Irish university experience is slipping, and going to get worse over time"', *Irish Times*, 22 June 2024.

Chapter 2

[1] The Protestant nationalist Stephen Gwynn said around 1911 that English opponents of Home Rule essentially believed that 'Ireland is unfit for self-government … asserting the special incapacity of Irishmen to undertake the task (*The case for Home Rule*, available at: https://celt.ucc.ie/published/E900030/text002.html (2 May 2025)). Winston Churchill once said that the Irish had 'a genius for conspiracy rather than government' (Fearghal McGarry, 'Taking Sides: Britain's involvement in the Irish Civil War', RTÉ, 11 May 2023, available at: https://www.rte.ie/player/movie/taking-sides-britain-and-the-civil-war-e1/395582504008 (2 May 2025)). His view of Ireland was far more complex and even affectionate than the crudity of this quote suggests; as a young man in 1896, he said that 'England has treated Ireland disgracefully in the past' and in 1912 he came to Belfast to support Home Rule, telling a crowd that 'this race – gifted, virtuous and brave, which has lived so long and endured so much should not, in view of her passionate desire, be shut out of the family of nations and should not be lost forever among indiscriminate multitudes of men' (Diarmaid Ferriter, 'Churchill Proceedings – "The Dev" and Mr. Churchill: An Irish nationalist's view of a complicated relationship', *Finest Hour*, available at: https://winstonchurchill.org/publications/finest-hour/finest-hour-145/churchill-proceedings-the-dev-and-mr-churchill-an-irish-nationalists-view-of-a-complicated-relationship/ (2 May 2025)); Paul Bew, 'What did Churchill really think about Ireland?', *Irish Times*, 8 February 2012.

Endnotes

[2] Sam McBride, 'Still reeling from Boris Johnson's betrayal, DUP founding member says he's questioning the Union', *News Letter*, 24 March 2021.

[3] Quoted in John Whyte, *Interpreting Northern Ireland* (Oxford, 1991), 15.

[4] The figures in question are not perfectly comparable due to methodological differences over such a long period, but the central point is fair – NILT 2023 data, available at: https://www.ark.ac.uk/nilt/2023/Political_Attitudes/IRBRIT.html (22 April 2025).

[5] Fergal Keane, *Wounds: a memoir of war & love* (Glasgow, 2017), 260.

[6] Robert W. White, *Ruairí Ó Brádaigh: the life and politics of an Irish revolutionary* (Bloomington, 2020), 107.

[7] Dervla Murphy, *A place apart* (Penguin, 1979), 11.

[8] Marc Mulholland, 'Faulkner, (Arthur) Brian Deane', *Dictionary of Irish Biography*, available at: https://www.dib.ie/biography/faulkner-arthur-brian-deane-a3021 (2 May 2025).

[9] *Hansard*, Orders of the day, vol. 457, 28 October 1948.

[10] William Beattie Smith, *The British state and the Northern Ireland crisis 1969–73: from violence to power-sharing* (Washington, DC, 2011), 76.

[11] Ferdinand Mount, 'Great sums of money' (book review), *London Review of Books* 43 (20) (21 October 2021).

[12] Paddy Devlin, *Yes, we have no bananas: outdoor relief in Belfast, 1920–39* (Newtownards, 1981), 22.

[13] Devlin, *Yes, we have no bananas*, 23.

[14] Anthony Alcock, *Understanding Ulster* (Lurgan, 1994), 76.

[15] *Hansard*, 'Address in reply to His Majesty's most gracious speech', vol. 48, cc. 5–56, 14 December 1921.

[16] *Hansard*, 'Northern Ireland (security)', Commons, 6 May 1987.

[17] Kieran Dineen, 'Fianna Fail leader Micheal Martin says he would not wear a poppy or funny socks if he replaces Leo Varadkar as taoiseach', *Irish Sun*, 28 December 2017.

[18] Padraig O'Malley, *Perils and prospects of a united Ireland* (Dublin, 2023), 338.

[19] Article 15.2 of the Irish Constitution states that 'Provision may however be made by law for the creation or recognition of subordinate legislatures'.

[20] Brendan O'Leary, *Making sense of a united Ireland: should it happen? How might it happen?* (Dublin, 2022), 17.

[21] John Hume, 'John Hume on the end of the unionist veto in Ulster', *London Review of Books* 11 (3) (2 February 1989).

[22] Gerry Moriarty, 'Trimble says Republic is sectarian and pathetic', *Irish Times*, 11 March 2002.

[23] 'Finding unity in diversity: John Hume talks to Professor Anthony Clare about what it means to be Irish', RTÉ, 6 February 1989, available at: https://www.rte.ie/archives/2019/0125/1025490-john-hume/ (22 April 2025).

[24] CSO, 'Census of Population 2022 – Summary results, migration and diversity', 30 May 2023, available at: https://www.cso.ie/en/releasesandpublications/ep/p-cpsr/censusofpopulation2022-summaryresults/migrationanddiversity/ (2 May 2025).

[25] John Hewitt, 'Conacre: a poem' (privately printed, 1943).

[26] Malachi O'Doherty, *Can Ireland be one?* (Dublin, 2022), 189.

[27] John Bruton, 'Full version of a 2016 speech by the late John Bruton the former Taoiseach: "The 1916 Easter Rising was not a just war"', *News Letter*, 6 February 2024.

[28] Martin Doyle, 'North stars: "the vitality of Northern Irish writing has always coincided with political upheaval"', *Irish Times*, 10 February 2024.
[29] Sam McBride, 'NI's broken NHS is killing people, and our populist politicians are overwhelmingly to blame', *Belfast Telegraph*, 3 June 2023.
[30] Business Consultancy Services, *Focus group research with Ukrainian guests and hosts*, July 2022, available at: https://www.executiveoffice-ni.gov.uk/sites/default/files/publications/execoffice/ukraine-focus-group-research-report.pdf (2 May 2025), 20. The problem is island-wide; Ukrainian refugees in the Republic have also been returning home for health treatment due to long waiting lists.
[31] Peter Donaghy, X, 24 February 2023, available at: https://x.com/peterdonaghy/status/1629071703195230209 (22 April 2025).
[32] Helen McGurk, 'Most people diagnosed with a less survivable cancer in Northern Ireland will die within one year, research reveals', *News Letter*, 15 January 2025.
[33] World Bank Group Health Nutrition and Population Statistics, 'Physicians (per 1,000 people)', available at: https://databank.worldbank.org/source/health-nutrition-and-population-statistics/Series/SH.MED.PHYS.ZS (22 April 2025).
[34] Technically, Northern Ireland has never been part of the NHS, but this is a distinction without a difference; it operates to NHS standards and principles, even if under the control of Stormont rather than the GB bureaucracy.
[35] Report in my possession, entitled *Benchmarking Northern Ireland healthcare performance – March 2024*.
[36] Department of Health, 'Life expectancy in Northern Ireland 2021–23: headline figures', 3 December 2024, available at: https://www.health-ni.gov.uk/news/life-expectancy-northern-ireland-2021-23-headline-figures (22 April 2025); Statista, 'Ireland: life expectancy at birth from 2012 to 2022, by gender', 5 November 2024, available at: https://www.statista.com/statistics/970773/life-expectancy-at-birth-in-ireland-by-gender/ (22 April 2025).
[37] World Population Review, 'PISA scores by country 2025', available at: https://worldpopulationreview.com/country-rankings/pisa-scores-by-country (22 April 2025).
[38] Jenni Ingram, Jamie Stiff, Stuart Cadwallader, Gabriel Lee and Heather Kayton, *PISA 2022: National report for Northern Ireland* (Belfast, 2023).
[39] Anne Devlin, Seamus McGuinness, Adele Bergin and Emer Smyth, 'Education across the island of Ireland: examining educational outcomes, earnings and intergenerational mobility', *Irish Studies in International Affairs* 34 (2) (2023), 30–47.
[40] UNICEF, *Child poverty in the midst of wealth*, Innocenti Report Card 18 (Florence, 2023), 8.
[41] O'Leary, *Making sense of a united Ireland*, 120.
[42] Keane, *Wounds*, 260.
[43] Ralph Hewitt, 'You're not welcome here, loyalist umbrella body tells Irish officials', *Belfast Telegraph*, 18 June 2021; Jonathan McCambridge, 'Well-known loyalist denied bail on firearms charges after Coveney security alert', *breakingnews.ie*, 11 June 2022, available at: https://www.breakingnews.ie/ireland/loyalist-denied-bail-after-court-told-weapons-and-ammunition-were-found-in-car-1318484.html (21 July 2025).
[44] Roger Scruton, *How to be a conservative* (London, 2014), 170.
[45] 'Union man: Nelson González talks to David Trimble MP', *Third Way* 19 (9) (1996), 18.

Endnotes

[46] UNDP, 'Human Development Index (HDI)', available at: https://hdr.undp.org/data-center/human-development-index#/indicies/HDI (22 April 2025).

[47] O'Malley, *Perils and prospects of a united Ireland*, 146.

[48] Jonathan Bardon, 'Covenant lecture', Northern Ireland Assembly, available at: https://www.niassembly.gov.uk/about-the-assembly/assembly-commission/perspectives/covenant-lecture/ (22 April 2025).

[49] Office for National Statistics, 'Regional economic activity by gross domestic product, UK: 1998 to 2022', 24 April 2024, available at: https://www.ons.gov.uk/economy/grossdomesticproductgdp/bulletins/regionaleconomicactivitybygrossdomesticproductuk/1998to2022 (22 April 2025); John Campbell, 'Northern Ireland's per-person GDP "similar to Poland"', BBC, 2 September 2024, available at: https://www.bbc.com/news/articles/c628r38nr2po.

[50] Statista, 'Ireland: gross domestic product (GDP) in current prices from 1989 to 2029', 8 November 2024, available at: https://www.statista.com/statistics/375217/gross-domestic-product-gdp-in-ireland/ (22 April 2025).

[51] John Oliver, *Working at Stormont* (Dublin, 1978), 43.

[52] Royal Commission on the Constitution 1969–1973, *Volume I report* (London, 1973), 395.

[53] John FitzGerald and Edgar L.W. Morgenroth, *The Northern Ireland economy: problems and prospects* (Dublin, 2019), 15.

[54] Robert Caro, *The power broker* (London, 2014; first published 1974), 124.

[55] O'Malley, *Perils and prospects of a united Ireland*, 173.

[56] Department of Foreign Affairs and Trade, 'Ireland and Britain: the Irish in Britain', available at: https://www.dfa.ie/media/dfa/alldfawebsitemedia/ourrolesandpolicies/ourwork/statevisit2014/The-irish-in-britain.pdf (22 April 2025).

[57] Hume, 'Finding unity in diversity'.

[58] Sean Fearon, 'Reunification – a roadmap to eco-social transformation on the island of Ireland', available at: https://znetwork.org/znetarticle/reunification-a-roadmap-to-eco-social-transformation-on-the-island-of-ireland/ (22 April 2025).

[59] Chris Dooley, *Redmond: a life undone* (Dublin, 2015), 310.

[60] United Nations, 'Ukraine: over 6 million refugees spread across Europe', available at: https://unric.org/en/ukraine-over-6-million-refugees-spread-across-europe/ (22 April 2025).

[61] St Patrick, 'A letter to the soldiers of Coroticus', available at: http://www.ancient-texts.org/library/celtic/ctexts/p02.html (22 April 2025).

[62] Marie Coleman, 'King's speech appealed to "all Irishmen ... to forgive and forget"', *Irish Times*, 25 May 2021.

Chapter 3

[1] Northern Ireland Government, *Why the border must be*, available at: https://cain.ulster.ac.uk/othelem/docs/nigov56.htm (24 July 2025).

[2] Northern Ireland Government, *Why the border must be*, available at: https://cain.ulster.ac.uk/othelem/docs/nigov56.htm (24 July 2025).

[3] Ulster's Solemn Covenant, 1912, available at: https://collections.nationalmuseumsni.org/object-belum-w2011-1265.

[4] NISRA, *Census 2021, Main statistics for Northern Ireland: Statistical Bulletin: Religion*, 22 September 2022, available at: https://www.nisra.gov.uk/system/files/statistics/census-2021-main-statistics-for-northern-ireland-phase-1-statistical-bulletin-religion.pdf (21 April 2025).

[5] Cormac Ó Gráda and Kevin O'Rourke, 'The Irish economy during the century after partition', *Economic History Review* 75 (2) (2022), 336–70.

[6] Janez Kren and Martina Lawless, *Structure of international goods trade for Ireland and Northern Ireland*, ESRI Survey and Statistical Report Series 117 (Dublin, 2023).

[7] *Hansard*, House of Commons statement, 10 November 1981, HC Deb, vol. 12, cc. 421–8.

[8] Quoted in *Hansard*, HC Deb, 11 November 1992, vol. 213, cc. 877–94.

[9] YouGov/Future of England Survey Results, Fieldwork: 30 May–4 June 2018, available at: https://d25d2506sfb94s.cloudfront.net/cumulus_uploads/document/8gzxmxtckl/FOE_England_June2018_Results_w.pdf (21 April 2025).

[10] Channel 4, 'C4 survey: UK would vote to remain in EU by majority of 54% to 46%', available at: https://www.channel4.com/press/news/c4-survey-uk-would-vote-remain-eu-majority-54-46-0 (2 May 2025).

[11] Matthew Smith, 'Most Conservative members would see party destroyed to achieve Brexit', YouGov, 18 June 2019, available at: https://yougov.co.uk/politics/articles/23849-most-conservative-members-would-see-party-destroye (21 April 2025).

[12] James Connolly, 'Labour and the proposed partition of Ireland', *Irish Worker*, 14 March 1914.

[13] Katy Hayward and Ben Rosher, 'Political identities and aspirations in Northern Ireland', Ark Research Update 155, June 2024, available at: https://www.ark.ac.uk/ARK/sites/default/files/2024-06/update155.pdf (21 April 2025).

[14] NISRA, *Census 2021, Main statistics for Northern Ireland: Statistical Bulletin: National identity*, 22 September 2022, available at: https://www.nisra.gov.uk/system/files/statistics/census-2021-main-statistics-for-northern-ireland-phase-1-statistical-bulletin-national-identity.pdf (21 April 2025).

[15] John Garry, Brendan O'Leary and Jamie Pow, 'Northern Ireland identity may serve as less adversarial for politically moderate Catholics and Protestants', *Irish Times*, 11 December 2023.

[16] CSO, 'Census of Population 2016 – Profile 8 Irish Travellers, ethnicity and religion', n.d., available at: https://www.cso.ie/en/releasesandpublications/ep/p-cp8iter/p8iter/p8rrc/ (21 April 2025).

[17] Patsy McGarry, 'Priest numbers in Dublin to fall 70 per cent in 20 years, report predicts', *Irish Times*, 11 November 2024.

[18] Garry et al., 'Northern Ireland identity may serve as less adversarial for politically moderate Catholics and Protestants'.

[19] Hayward and Rosher, 'Political identities and aspirations in Northern Ireland'.

[20] NISRA, *Census 2021, Main statistics for Northern Ireland: Statistical Bulletin: Passports held*, 22 September 2022, available at: https://www.nisra.gov.uk/system/files/statistics/census-2021-main-statistics-for-northern-ireland-phase-1-statistical-bulletin-passports-held.pdf (21 April 2025).

[21] Garry et al., 'Public attitudes to Irish unification', 247–87.

[22] Fiachra Ó Cionnaith, 'Housing, homelessness biggest issue for Election 2024 voters', RTÉ, 30 November 2024, available at: https://www.rte.ie/news/election-24/2024/1130/1483888-election-age-gender/ (21 April 2025).

Endnotes

[23] Loscher, 'Irish Times/ARINS poll: support for United Ireland is strong, but debate on costs and compromises to come first'.

[24] Manfred Kuechler, 'The road to German unity: mass sentiment in East and West Germany', *Public Opinion Quarterly* 56 (1) (1992), 53–76.

[25] Garry et al., 'Public attitudes to Irish unification'.

[26] Pat Leahy, 'Southern voters would consider big changes to institutions in a united Ireland', *Irish Times*, 7 March 2025.

[27] John Garry, Brendan O'Leary and Jamie Pow, 'Would a united Ireland require a new constitution?', *Irish Times*, 9 December 2023.

[28] Council of Europe, *Monitoring of the application of the European Charter of Local Self-government in Ireland*, available at: https://rm.coe.int/cg-2023-45-17prov-en-monitoring-of-the-application-of-the-european-cha/1680acd809%20e (21 April 2025).

[29] Seanín Graham, 'Threat of violence rises as loyalists vent frustrations with protocol', *Irish Times*, 31 March 2022.

[30] FitzGerald and Morgenroth, 'Northern Ireland subvention'.

[31] Dáil Éireann debate, 21 March 2024, question 129.

[32] Maureen O'Reilly, Annmarie O'Kane and Rose Tierney, *A study into the current conditions of the island of Ireland labour market, and challenges and opportunities for effective operation for workers and businesses across the island*, Centre for Cross Border Cooperation (Armagh, 2024).

[33] Kren and Lawless, *Structure of international goods trade for Ireland and Northern Ireland*.

[34] Martina Lawless, *Cross-border trade in services*, ESRI Research Series 129 (Dublin, 2021).

[35] Joint Committee on the Implementation of the Good Friday Agreement, *Perspectives on constitutional change: finance and economics*, 14 July 2024, available at: https://www.oireachtas.ie/en/press-centre/press-releases/20240716-joint-committee-on-the-implementation-of-the-good-friday-agreement-publishes-report-perspectives-on-constitutional-change-finance-and-economics/ (21 April 2025).

[36] Department of Communities, *The Northern Ireland poverty and income inequality report (2022/23)*, 27 March 2024, available at: https://www.communities-ni.gov.uk/news/northern-ireland-poverty-and-income-inequality-report-2022-23-released (21 April 2025).

[37] Bertrand Maître, Helen Russell, Anousheh Alamir and Eva Slevin, *Child poverty on the island of Ireland*, ESRI Research Series 199 (Dublin, 2025).

[38] STADA health report 2024, *Satisfaction with health systems continues to decline*, available at: https://www.stada.com/media/9097/stada_health-report_en_final.pdf (21 April 2025).

[39] Department of Health, *Sláintecare Progress Report 2021–2023*, 6, available at: https://www.lenus.ie/handle/10147/641495?show=full (21 April 2025).

[40] Priscilla Lynch, 'North and South: the general practice dilemma', *Medical Independent*, 30 March 2024, available at: https://www.medicalindependent.ie/in-the-news/news-features/north-and-south-the-general-practice-dilemma/ (21 April 2025).

[41] Jimmy Larsen and Paul Moran, *A review of private health insurance 2023*, Health Insurance Authority, available at: https://www.hia.ie/sites/default/files/2024-01/hia-consumer-survey-2023-final_0.pdf (21 April 2025).

[42] Oireachtas Joint Committee on the Implementation of the Good Friday Agreement debate, 2 May 2024, available at: https://www.oireachtas.ie/en/debates/debate/joint_committee_on_the_implementation_of_the_good_friday_agreement/2024-05-02/ (21 April 2025).

[43] Oireachtas Joint Committee on the Implementation of the Good Friday Agreement debate, 2 May 2024.

[44] New decade, new approach, 2020, available at: assets.gov.ie/static/documents/new-decade-new-approach-8559e5c6-5ee5-40e8-9ba1-b40cfba715c3.pdf.

Chapter 4

[1] Karl Marx, *The 18th Brumaire of Louis Bonaparte* (Cabin John, MD, 2008; first published 1852), 15.

[2] Andrew Gailey, *Crying in the wilderness: Jack Sayers – a liberal editor in Ulster, 1939–69* (Liverpool, 1995), 136.

[3] Paddy Devlin, *Straight left* (Newtownards, 1993), 80.

[4] A.T.Q. Stewart, *The narrow ground* (Devizes, 1986; first published 1977), 183.

[5] Mary Gilmartin and Clíodhna Murphy, 'A small country with a huge diaspora, Ireland navigates its new status as an immigration hub', *Migration Information Source*, 5 June 2024, available at: https://www.migrationpolicy.org/article/ireland-diaspora-immigration (21 April 2025).

[6] Katy Hayward and Paula Devine, 'Attitudes to immigration in Northern Ireland', *Research Update*, Ark, February 2025, available at: https://www.ark.ac.uk/ARK/sites/default/files/2025-03/update160.pdf (2 May 2025).

[7] Stewart, *The narrow ground*, 113.

[8] *BBC News*, 'In full: Queen's Ireland state banquet speech', available at: https://www.bbc.com/news/world-europe-13450099 (2 May 2025).

[9] Murphy, *A place apart*, 47 (emphasis in original).

[10] Donnchadh Ó Corráin, 'Prehistoric and Early Christian Ireland' in R.F. Foster (ed.), *The Oxford history of Ireland* (Oxford, 1989), 6.

[11] 'Army Estimates, 1956–57: Part of Orders of the Day – Supply – in the House of Commons at 12:00 am on 1 March 1956', available at: https://www.theyworkforyou.com/debates/?id=1956-03-01a.1427.0 (21 April 2025).

[12] The Northern Ireland Constitution Act 1973 said that Northern Ireland couldn't leave the Union 'without the consent of the majority of the people of Northern Ireland voting in a [border] poll'. The Ireland Act 1949 had said Northern Ireland couldn't leave without the Stormont parliament's consent. Whatever the formulation, from the outset it was clear that Northern Ireland's retention within the Union depended on that being the wish of the majority.

[13] While the Famine involved a misguidedly unshakeable belief in laissez-faire economics as well as episodes of malevolence, such a human calamity would have been unthinkable in Britain.

[14] Devlin, *Yes, we have no bananas*, 15.

[15] Conor O'Clery, 'Whatever you say, on mature recollection, say nothing', *Irish Times*, 16 October 1999.

Endnotes

[16] *BBC News*, 'Ian Paisley: in quotes', 12 September 2014, available at: https://www.bbc.co.uk/news/uk-northern-ireland-29171017 (21 April 2025).
[17] Whyte, *Interpreting Northern Ireland*, 155.
[18] Whyte, *Interpreting Northern Ireland*, 162.
[19] 'Unionists were right to be fearful that Home Rule meant Rome Rule, admits Sinn Fein's Mary Lou McDonald', *Belfast Telegraph*, 22 June 2020.
[20] O'Malley, *Perils and prospects of a united Ireland*, 281.
[21] John Hedges, 'Irish and British governments should stand up to "negative anti-Agreement axis"', *An Phoblacht*, 11 September 2014.
[22] O'Malley, *Perils and prospects of a united Ireland*, 205.
[23] Gary Murphy, *In search of the promised land: the politics of post-war Ireland* (Cork, 2009), 245.
[24] John Campbell, 'United Ireland would cost €8bn to €20bn a year, study suggests', BBC, 4 April 2024, available at: https://www.bbc.co.uk/news/uk-northern-ireland-68723508 (21 April 2025).
[25] John Campbell, 'New study challenges united Ireland cost', BBC, 25 May 2024, available at: https://www.bbc.co.uk/news/articles/cyee9y1j8gwo (21 April 2025).
[26] Scottish Government, 'Scottish government position on pensions in an independent Scotland: FOI release', 16 December 2023, available at: https://www.gov.scot/publications/scottish-government-position-on-pensions-in-an-independent-scotland-foi-release/ (21 April 2025).
[27] David Eiser, 'Who pays the state pension in an independent Scotland?', Fraser of Allander Institute, 5 February 2022, available at: https://fraserofallander.org/who-pays-the-state-pension-in-an-independent-scotland/ (21 April 2025).
[28] Whyte, *Interpreting Northern Ireland*, 230.
[29] Whyte, *Interpreting Northern Ireland*, 232.
[30] O'Malley, *Perils and prospects of a united Ireland*, 183.
[31] Niall O'Connor, 'Crisis meeting among Defence Forces chiefs over ships going to sea without working guns', *The Journal*, 25 January 2025, available at: https://www.thejournal.ie/high-level-crisis-meeting-among-defence-forces-chiefs-as-naval-gun-crisis-deepens-6602434-Jan2025/ (21 April 2025).
[32] O'Doherty, *Can Ireland be one?*, 181.
[33] RTÉ, 'Lowry helped O'Brien get mobile licence', 22 March 2011, available at: https://www.rte.ie/news/2011/0322/298935-moriarty_background/ (21 April 2025).
[34] NISRA, *Quarterly employment survey*, available at: https://www.nisra.gov.uk/statistics/labour-market-and-social-welfare/quarterly-employment-survey (21 April 2025).
[35] Paul Gosling, *A new Ireland. A new Union: a new society. A ten year plan* (2018), 24, available at: https://cain.ulster.ac.uk/issues/unification/2020-05-11_Gosling_New-Ireland.pdf (21 April 2025).
[36] Gosling, *A new Ireland*, 102.
[37] O'Malley, *Perils and prospects of a united Ireland*, 304; Pat Leahy, 'Large majority of voters favour a united Ireland, poll finds', *Irish Times*, 11 December 2021.
[38] 'Programme for Government Indicator 5: Satisfaction with health and social care', available at: https://www.health-ni.gov.uk/sites/default/files/publications/health/pfg-5_1.pdf (21 April 2025).
[39] Laura Lynott, 'Private school fees rising due to "inflation and a lack of government funding" with parents now paying over €10,000 at one school', *Irish Indepen-*

dent, 8 January 2024; Methodist College Belfast, 'Fees', available at: https://www.methody.org/admissions/fees (21 April 2025).
[40] 'Ireland Toll Calculator – M50 toll, toll fees, and Eflow', available at: https://tollguru.com/toll-calculator-ireland (22 April 2025).
[41] While many people in the Republic now receive BBC services without paying for them, this is unlikely to continue. Some of this comes from the spillover of signal broadcast in or into Northern Ireland, which would no longer be necessary. More significantly, in the digital age geo-blocking services are simpler and already the BBC is exploring doing this for the Republic due to rights issues around music, film and sport.
[42] Met Éireann, 'Candidate information booklet', available at: https://www.met.ie/cms/assets/uploads/2023/10/Forecaster-CANDIDATE-INFORMATION-BOOKLET-2023_final.pdf (22 April 2025); Met Office, *Equality, diversity & inclusion annual report 2021–2022*, available at: https://www.metoffice.gov.uk/binaries/content/assets/metofficegovuk/pdf/about-us/careers/edi-progress-report-v9.pdf (22 April 2025).
[43] World Meter, 'GDP by country', available at: https://www.worldometers.info/gdp/gdp-by-country/ (2 May 2025).
[44] Numbeo, 'Cost of living comparison between Dublin and Belfast', available at: https://www.numbeo.com (22 April 2025).
[45] Ailbhe Conneely, 'Rising cost of living impacting child poverty levels – ESRI', RTÉ, 16 January 2025, available at: https://www.rte.ie/news/2025/0116/1491102-income-level-esri/ (22 April 2025).
[46] Central Bank of Ireland, 'Economic Letter: Is Ireland really the most prosperous country in Europe?', 4 February 2021, available at: https://www.centralbank.ie/news/article/press-release-economic-letter-is-ireland-really-the-most-prosperous-country-in-europe-04-january-2021 (22 April 2025).

Postscript

[1] O'Malley, *Perils and prospects of a united Ireland*, 283.
[2] Quoted in John Horne, Carson's Farewell to Ulster, Creative Centenaries, May 2021, available at: https://www.creativecentenaries.org/blog/carson-s-farewell-to-ulster (21 July 2025).

Further reading

Aughey, Arthur, 'The State of the Union: Lessons for a shared, prosperous future' (Policy Exchange, 2018). Available online at: https://policyexchange.org.uk/wp-content/uploads/2018/05/The-State-of-the-Union.pdf (accessed 22 July 2025).

Bergin, A., McGuinness, S. and Banahan, C., 'Economic overview of Ireland and Northern Ireland', ESRI Research Series 203 (2025), Dublin: ESRI. Available online at: https://doi.org/10.26504/rs203 (accessed 22 July 2025).

Cochrane, Feargal, *Northern Ireland: The Fragile Peace* (Yale University Press, 2021).

Connolly, Frank, *United Nation: The Case for Integrating Ireland* (Dublin: Gill Books, 2022).

Edwards, Aaron, *A People Under Siege: The Unionists of Northern Ireland, from Partition to Brexit and Beyond* (Dublin: Merrion Press, 2023).

Foster, R.F. (ed.), *The Oxford History of Ireland* (Oxford: Oxford University Press, 2001).

Gosling, Paul, *A New Ireland. A New Union: A New Society. A Ten Year Plan* (self-published, 2018. Available online at: https://cain.ulster.ac.uk/issues/unification/2020-05-11_Gosling_New-Ireland.pdf (accessed 22 July 2025).

Hall, Amanda, *Strained Peace: Northern Ireland from Good Friday to Brexit* (Liverpool: Liverpool University Press, 2024).

Hayward, Katy, *What Do We Know and What Should We Do About the Irish Border?* (California: Sage Publishing, 2021).

Lynch, Robert, *The Partition of Ireland 1918–1925* (Cambridge: Cambridge University Press, 2019).

McBride, Sam, *Burned: The Inside Story of the 'Cash-for-Ash' Scandal and Northern Ireland's Secretive New Elite* (Dublin: Merrion Press, 2019).

McKay, Susan, *Northern Protestants: On Shifting Ground* (Newtownards: Blackstaff Press, 2021).

McKay, Susan, *Protestants: An Unsettled People* (Newtownards: Blackstaff Press, 2000).

Murphy, Dervla, *A Place Apart* (London: Penguin, 1979).

O'Doherty, Malachi, *How to Fix Northern Ireland* (London: Atlantic Books, 2023).

O'Doherty, Malachi, *Can Ireland be one?* (Dublin, 2022).

O'Leary, Brendan, *Making Sense of a United Ireland: Should it happen? How might it happen?* (Dublin: Sandycove, 2020).

O'Malley, Padraig, *Perils and Prospects of a United Ireland* (Dublin: The Lilliput Press, 2023).

Patterson, Henry and Kaufmann, Eric, *Unionism and Orangeism in Northern Ireland Since 1945: The Decline of the Loyal Family* (Manchester: Manchester University Press, 2007).

Stewart, A.T.Q., *The Narrow Ground* (Belfast: The Pretani Press, 1977).

Townshend, Charles, *The Partition: Ireland Divided 1885-1925* (London: Penguin UK, 2021).

Whitten, Lisa Claire, *Brexit and the Northern Ireland Constitution* (Oxford: Oxford University Press, 2023).

Whyte, John, *Interpreting Northern Ireland* (Oxford: Clarendon Press, 1991).

Acknowledgements

The idea behind this book was brilliant, but it wasn't ours. If you enjoyed reading this volume as much as we enjoyed writing it, the credit for the concept goes to Pauric Dempsey at the University of Notre Dame. He approached each of us two years ago with a proposal that was incredibly simple but that doesn't seem to have occurred to anyone before.

What attracted us to the project was the integrity of the idea – that there should exist a concise work accessible to anyone on this island setting out the best arguments for and against Irish unity.

As part of the ARINS project, the idea was to take some of the work of academics and convey it in a straightforward way to the general reader. It is important that academics examine these issues, but they are too important to remain within the academy.

Behind any book lie many names beyond those on the cover. Ruth Hegarty at the Royal Irish Academy was the driving force behind the project, skilfully managing two authors and the concept of an academic press publishing what is a non-academic book on a complex and controversial subject.

Fiona Dunne, our editor at the Royal Irish Academy, dealt patiently with the evolving nature of the book, gently keeping us to deadlines and steering the work towards completion.

Aifric Downey assisted in innumerable practical ways, making arrangements and suggestions that helped make the book what it is. If you listened to the audiobook version, Noel Storey at Beacon Studios is the expert sound engineer who, with proficiency and humour, helped us translate words on a page into words in your ear.

Fergus Boylan had immediate enthusiasm for the idea of lightening what could be seen as a heavy topic with a satirical artist's light touch. His ideas for cartoons were brilliant; our only regret is that more of them couldn't be included.

Copyeditor Brendan O'Brien did a magnificent job of tidying up the text, going beyond the call of duty in clarifying both the text and our thinking.

For and against a united Ireland

Fidelma Slattery expertly laid out the text and helped draw up some of the charts. Our particular thanks to Professor John FitzGerald, Adele Bergin and Paul Nolan for help in creating and reviewing several charts.

Our thanks to designer Graham Thew for the striking cover, and to indexer Lisa Scholey for helping you to find your way around.

Our thanks also go to the Royal Irish Academy's peer reviewers who ensured that, while this isn't an academic book, it benefited from robust internal criticism before reaching your hands.

Fintan would like to thank Natasha Fairweather and Catriona Crowe.

Sam would like to thank Stephen Adams, who generously gave him the use of a cottage to write in secluded peace while looking out at the Irish border. Much of his text was written there or at the Tyrone Guthrie Centre in Annaghmakerrig, a unique place of cross-border creativity where painters, musicians, writers and other artists come together.

Sam would also like to thank two people without whom he would never have been able to write: his longsuffering wife, Anna – who, after *Burned*, knew just how much work a book could involve – and his editor at the *Belfast Telegraph*, Eoin Brannigan, who immediately agreed to him taking part in the project. Sam is also appreciative of the many people who spoke to him unattributably while researching the book: politicians, academics, experts in various fields, and others.

Our final thanks go to you, the reader, because without readers, books either would not exist or would be pointless. Whatever your view, whatever your background, and wherever you live, thank you for your interest in what we have written.

Index

A

abortion, 36, 84
Act of Union, 36–7, 113
Adams, Gerry, 71, 125
agriculture, 38, 78, 80
Alcock, Antony, 41–2
Alliance Party, 58, 124
Amhrán na bhFiann, 18, 92
Anglicanism, 77, 78
Anglo-Irish Agreement, 96
Anglo-Irish Treaty, 3, 116
anthems, 14, 16–18, 89, 92, 140
ARINS, 10, 11, 14, 16–17, 18, 24, 26, 84, 86, 89–90, 93
arts, 49
Aughey, Arthur, 154

B

Bardon, Jonathan, 63–4
BBC, 49, 88, 110, 143
Belfast, 4, 38, 41, 62–4, 71, 79, 94, 96–8, 118, 120, 143, 147
Belfast Agreement, 6, 8, 12, 17–18, 24, 43, 56, 60, 67, 81, 93, 98, 106, 117, 149
Belfast Telegraph, 112, 123, 143
Bergin, Adele, 28
Bevin, Ernest, 2
Birnie, Esmond, 66
Blythe, Ernest, 121
border control, 62
border crossings, 96–7, 124
border poll, 12–15, 58–9, 68, 94–5, 106, 110–11, 117, 134–7, 150–3
Borooah, Vani, 28
Brady, Hugh, 30–1
brain drain, 29, 30
brewing, 79
Brexit, 21, 42, 49, 70, 81–4, 87, 96–7, 100, 110–11, 123, 137–8, 148, 149–50, 153
British Empire, 34, 40, 114–15
British identity, 13, 16–18, 36, 78, 84, 88–9, 152
Brooke, Basil, Viscount Brookeborough, 7, 39, 74–5, 76
Brooke, Peter, 81
Bruton, John, 48
Buckley, Anthony, 35
Bunreacht na hÉireann *see* Constitution of Ireland

C

carbon-free economy, 31, 98
Carson, Edward, 37, 42, 121, 154
Carthy, Matt, 2
'cash for ash' scandal, 65
Catholicism
    Catholic Church, 5, 26, 28, 29, 45, 104, 116, 121
    Catholic hospitals, 26
    Catholic schools, 28, 29
    discrimination against Catholics, 39, 41, 116
    and Home Rule, 46, 121
    and the Irish Constitution, 4–5, 6–7
    and Irish identity, 4–5, 6–7, 36, 84–7
    in Northern Ireland, 4, 8, 28, 35–6, 39, 41, 77–8, 84, 86, 114, 116, 118, 122–3, 152
    in the Republic of Ireland, 4–5, 6–7, 26, 29, 38, 45, 75, 84, 85, 121
censorship, 75
census data, 13, 78, 84
Charles III, 48
child poverty, 56, 100–1

childcare, 31, 85, 90
Church of Ireland, 78
Churchill, Sir Winston, 40
citizens' assemblies, 92, 147
citizenship, 17, 84
civil rights, 112
civil service, 40, 43, 139
civil society, 31
Clark, Sir George, 39
climate change, 14, 31, 69, 90, 154
Cold War, 115
comedy, 88
Common Travel Area, 144
Commonwealth, 16, 89, 140, 144
company registration, 145
Congress of Local and Regional Authorities, 93–4
Connolly, James, 83, 128
conservation organisations, 144
Conservative Party, 49, 80–3, 153–4
conservatism, 41, 49, 76, 80–3
Constitution of Ireland, 4–7, 14, 15–16, 43, 86, 93, 120
contraception, 75
Cork, 79, 94, 98, 143
corruption, 138
cost of living, 90, 101, 147
courts, 14
Coveney, Simon, 58
Covid-19 pandemic, 54, 68, 145
Craig, James, 4, 37
cricket, 63, 70
crime, 62, 90
Cromwell, Oliver, 115
Cú Chulainn, 118
currency, 48, 110, 119, 132–3
cybersecurity, 136, 145

D

D-Day, 115
Dáil Éireann, 44, 85, 139, 154
data centres, 69
de Valera, Éamon, 44, 71, 126
defence, 14, 135–6, 137

Democratic Unionist Party (DUP), 34, 56, 82, 124, 154
Derry, 62, 112
Devlin, Paddy, 112, 118
devolution, 4, 14–16, 34, 42–3, 89, 93–4, 115, 116, 139–40
diaspora, 6, 66–7, 113–14
discrimination, 39, 41, 46, 85, 116, 136
disinformation, 12
diversity, 6, 15, 45–6, 63, 85–6
divorce, 5, 75
domestic violence, 85
Donaghy, Peter, 52
Doyle, John, 23, 131
Doyle, Oran, 6
Drennan, William, 36
drug smuggling, 62
Dublin, 79, 94, 97, 98, 143, 147
Dublin Metropolitan Police (DMP), 122

E

Easter Rising, 48, 70
economic growth, 96–8, 132, 148
economies of scale, 63, 98
economy, 18–21, 61, 63–5, 70, 76, 78–80, 90, 96–8, 117, 125–33, 138–9, 144
education, 27–31, 32, 56–7, 61, 97, 104–6, 107, 111, 124, 141, 151
educational migration, 28–9, 30
Eisenhower, Dwight, 115
Eiser, David, 132
electricity, 62, 69
Elizabeth II, 48, 49, 113
emblems, 14, 16–18, 47, 89, 92, 118–19
emigration, 88
employment, 39, 79–80, 85, 97, 98, 136, 139, 145–7
energy, 21, 62, 69, 98
England, 21, 40, 49, 52, 82–3, 85, 88, 119, 129, 133, 148

Index

environment, 68–9, 144
European Commission, 30
European identity, 86–7
European Union, 14, 61, 66, 68, 80–2, 86–7, 99, 123, 125, 137–9, 144; *see also* Brexit
Ewart, William, 79
expenditure, 19, 21, 94, 129

F

Famine, 40–1, 115
Farage, Nigel, 131
Fearon, Seán, 69
federalism, 44
First World War, 4, 34, 70
Fitt, Gerry, 2
FitzGerald, Garret, 4–5, 121
FitzGerald, John, 19, 20, 96, 105, 129, 131
Fitzpatrick, Ciara, 22
Five Eyes network, 59
flags, 14, 16–18, 89, 92, 118, 136, 140
food production, 78, 79, 80
foreign direct investment, 48, 60, 98
foreign policy, 14
Foster, Arlene, 47
fuel smuggling, 62

G

Gaelic Athletic Association (GAA), 17, 124
Garda Síochána, 12, 46, 95
Garry, John, 24, 86
GCHQ, 145
GCSE, 30, 56
gender, 85, 121
general practitioners (GPs), 23, 103
George V, 71
Germany, 66, 90–2, 106, 125–6, 149
Givan, Paul, 56, 141
Glasnevin Cemetery, 121
global financial crisis, 149
Good Friday Agreement *see* Belfast Agreement
Gosling, Paul, 139
Graham, Sir Clarence, 39
Great Depression, 79
Green Party (Ireland), 69
Griffith, Arthur, 2
Group of Seven (G7), 144
guns, 12, 135

H

Harris, Drew, 46
Harvey, Colin, 5
Haughey, Charlie, 138
Hayward, Katy, 86
Health Service Executive (HSE), 24, 27
healthcare, 14, 22–7, 31–2, 50–5, 62–3, 90, 97, 101–4, 107, 140–1, 151
Heenan, Deirdre, 26
Henry Ford & Sons, 79
Hewitt, John, 47
high kings, 3
higher education, 28–9, 30–1, 56
holiday entitlements, 147
Hogan, Gerard, 6
Home Rule, 4, 34, 63–4, 69, 76–7, 121
homosexuality, 36, 84–5, 121
Honohan, Patrick, 147
housing, 21, 31, 39, 80, 90, 144–5
Human Development Index, 60–1
Hume, John, 16, 18, 45, 67
Hutch, Gerry, 138

I

identity, 6, 13, 16–18, 36, 44, 78, 83–9, 148, 152
immigration, 46, 71, 90, 112, 117, 144
incomes, 18, 147
Independent Reporting Commission, 11
industry, 38, 63–4, 78–80, 118
inequalities, 61, 85, 99, 143

inflation, 147
infrastructure, 14, 21, 31, 43, 61, 62, 98, 117, 126, 151
integration, 14–16
intelligence services, 59
InterTrade Ireland, 97
Ireland's Future, 24
Irish Civil War, 38
Irish Defence Forces, 12, 135–6
Irish Free State, 3–4, 20, 37, 99–100, 129
Irish Guards, 119
Irish identity, 6, 13, 16–18, 36, 83–7, 152
Irish Independent, 19–20
Irish language, 13–14, 88, 124, 136
Irish Republican Army (IRA), 37–8, 59, 70, 116, 118, 122
Irish Sea border, 81, 123–4, 138
Irish Times, 2, 11, 14, 16–17, 18, 84, 86, 89–90, 93
Irish Women's Liberation Movement, 85
Irvine, Winston, 58
Israel, 29, 35, 67, 128
ITV, 88

J

Jackson, Alvin, 76
Jennings, Ivor, 5
Jesuit Order, 6
Johnson, Boris, 81
Johnson, Thomas, 121

K

Keane, Fergal, 38
Kearns, Leo, 26
Knox, Colin, 28

L

Labour Party (UK), 49, 54, 154
Lanyon, H.O., 63
laws, 14, 81, 119, 145

Leaving Certificate, 30
Lemass, Sean, 43
life expectancy, 24, 54–5
linen industry, 38, 63, 79–80
literature, 75, 88
Little-Pengelly, Emma, 124
living standards, 16, 21, 129, 131, 147
local government, 93–4
Londonderry, 62, 112
Lough Neagh, 69
Lowry, Michael, 138
loyalist paramilitaries, 10–12, 35, 47, 58–60, 94–6, 135

M

MacBride, Seán, 2
McCracken, Henry Joy, 36
McDonald, Mary Lou, 121
McEvoy, Joanne, 23
McGarry, Tim, 68
McGuinness, Seamus, 28
McKay, Sean, 54
Maginess, Brian, 39, 74–5
Martin, Micheál, 43
Marx, Karl, 111
Matthews, Anne, 26
May, Theresa, 81
means-testing, 22, 100–1
media, 42, 48–9, 75, 88, 111, 143
Met Éireann, 144
Met Office, 143–4
Methodism, 78
middle classes, 105–6
Molyneaux, Jim, 42
Montgomery, Bernard, 115
Moore, Thomas, 119
Morgenroth, Edgar, 19, 20, 96, 131
Mount, Ferdinand, 41
multiculturalism, 85–6, 119
multinationals, 96, 120, 128
Murphy, Dervla, 38, 58, 114
Murray, Joseph, 121
music, 88

Index

N

national debt, 20, 98–100, 129
National Health Service (NHS), 23–4, 50–5, 103–4, 107, 140–1
national symbols, 14, 16–18, 47, 89, 92, 118–19
nationalism
   English, 40
   Irish, 2–4, 6–8, 34–7, 39, 47–8, 58–60, 69–70, 76, 83–4, 95, 121, 123, 137, 150–2
   Scottish, 2, 40, 132, 153
   Welsh, 2, 40
NATO, 135
neutrality, 115, 137
New Decade, New Approach deal, 105–6
Northern Ireland Life and Times (NILT) surveys, 84, 86–7
Northern Ireland Protocol, 81, 96, 125, 144
Northern Ireland Women's Movement, 85
Northern Irish identity, 84, 87

O

Occupied Territories Bill, 128
O'Doherty, Malachi, 136
O'Flanagan, Fr. Michael, 2
O'Hanlon, W.M., 41
O'Leary, Brendan, 24, 44, 58, 86
Oliver, John, 64–5
O'Malley, Padraig, 153
O'Neill, Michelle, 124
Orange Order, 39, 125
Orme, Alan, 54
O'Sullivan, Charles, 22

P

Paisley, Ian, 34, 121
Palestine, 35, 128
partition, 2–5, 34, 37–8, 42, 74–6, 78, 83–4, 110, 116–18, 135, 152
passports, 87, 124
patriarchy, 85
Patrick, Saint, 70–1
Pearse, Patrick, 71
Penal Laws, 6
pensions, 20–1, 22, 98–9, 131–3, 147
people trafficking, 62
Plantation of Ulster, 113, 118
pluralism, 29, 45–8, 83, 87, 150
Police Service of Northern Ireland (PSNI), 12, 14, 43, 123, 124, 139
policing, 12, 14, 43, 46, 58, 95, 112, 122, 123, 139
political institutions, 13–16, 43–4, 93–4
popular culture, 88
popular sovereignty, 5, 10
populism, 52, 65
postal service, 43, 145
poverty, 41, 56, 100–1, 107
Pow, Jamie, 86
power-sharing, 14, 52, 56, 123, 140
Presbyterianism, 36–7, 63, 77, 78
primary education, 28, 29, 104
private healthcare, 26, 27, 50, 103
productivity, 27–8, 104, 105
Protestant Action Force (PAF), 96
Protestantism
   Anglicanism, 77, 78
   and British identity, 17, 36, 47, 78, 84
   and Home Rule, 46, 76–7, 121
   and Irish identity, 83–7
   Methodism, 78
   and nationalism, 36–7, 121
   in Northern Ireland, 4–5, 15, 17, 28, 35–8, 41, 47, 76–8, 83–7, 95–6, 105–6, 114
   Presbyterianism, 36–7, 63, 77, 78
   Protestant schools, 28, 29
   in the Republic of Ireland, 4, 29, 121–2, 152
public borrowing, 21, 67, 100
Public Only Consultant Contract, 103

public sector wages, 19, 131, 139, 144, 147
public services, 14, 64, 126, 129, 140, 147
public transport, 31, 98, 145, 151

Q

quality of life, 61

R

railways, 62, 97, 98, 145
Red Hand of Ulster, 17
Redmond, John, 69–70
refugees, 50, 70
religious education, 29
revenues, 19, 97, 120, 126–8
risk, 46, 61, 110, 119–22, 153
roads, 62, 97, 143
Rose, Richard, 36
Rosher, Ben, 86
Royal Air Force, 135
Royal Family, 48, 66, 88, 115, 119
Royal Irish Constabulary (RIC), 122
Royal Irish Regiment, 119
Royal Navy, 135
Royal Ulster Constabulary (RUC), 46, 112
Royal Ulster Rifles, 115
RTÉ, 49, 88, 143
rugby, 63, 70
Russia, 149
Ryan, James, 126

S

same-sex marriage, 84
Sayers, Jack, 112
Scotland, 2, 3, 20, 40, 88, 100, 114, 116, 118–19, 131–3, 148, 153
Scottish National Party (SNP), 131
Scruton, Roger, 59
Second World War, 4, 75, 115
secondary education, 28, 29, 56, 104

sectarianism, 11, 36–9, 41, 59, 70, 104, 116, 121–3
services, export of, 97
1798 Rebellion, 36
sexuality, 36, 84–5, 121
shipbuilding, 38, 64, 79–80
Sinn Féin, 2, 20, 24, 48, 60, 121, 123–5, 128–30, 134, 140, 147, 154
Sláintecare, 55, 103–4
Smyth, Austin, 54
soccer, 17, 42, 63, 88, 116, 139
Social Democratic and Labour Party (SDLP), 2, 112, 123, 134
social insurance contributions, 20, 131
social media, 12
social welfare, 14, 19, 21, 32, 98, 100–1, 107, 129, 147
sovereign wealth fund, 61, 62, 128
Soviet Union, 149
sport, 17, 42, 63, 70, 88, 92, 116, 124, 139
Stewart, A.T.Q., 112, 113
Stormont, 37, 43, 50–2, 65, 69, 74, 124, 139–40
Sturgeon, Nicola, 153
subvention, 19, 65, 66, 99, 129–30, 135–6, 147
Sunday Business Post, 18, 20
Sunningdale Agreement, 7

T

tariffs, 128
taxation, 14, 19–22, 48, 60, 82, 89, 98, 125–8, 129, 132–3, 140
textile industry, 38, 63, 79–80
Thatcher, Margaret, 81
Thompson, Wallace, 34
Todd, Jennifer, 23, 30
toll roads, 143
Tone, Theobald Wolfe, 36
Topping, Walter, 74
tourism, 48, 62
trade, 62, 70, 81, 96, 97–8, 107, 110, 138, 144, 149

Index

trade unions, 88
Traditional Unionist Voice (TUV), 123
transport, 21, 31, 62, 90, 98, 143, 145, 151
Tricolour, 17, 89, 92
Trimble, David, 45, 60, 122
Troubles, 36, 39, 45, 47, 58, 67, 68, 112, 125, 133, 149
Trump, Donald, 87, 106, 126, 128, 134, 149

U

Ukraine, 50, 70
Ulster Covenant, 64, 76–7, 124
Ulster Defence Association (UDA), 59
Ulster Unionist Party (UUP), 66, 96
Ulster Volunteer Force (UVF), 47, 58, 59, 96, 134
uncertainty, 119–20, 130, 132, 137
unemployment, 41, 145
unionism, 4, 17, 34–7, 39, 41–2, 45–8, 58–60, 65, 74, 80–4, 95–6, 117–18, 121–5, 134–7, 150–4
Unionist Party, 39
United Irishmen, 36

United Nations Security Council, 144
United States, 59, 60, 66–7, 87, 99, 106, 113–15, 126–8, 134, 149
unity referendum *see* border poll
universities, 28–9, 30–1, 48, 56, 119
urbanisation, 80

V

violence, 10–13, 32, 58–60, 94–6, 111–13, 133–6

W

waiting lists, 24, 26, 50–2, 54
Wales, 2, 20, 40, 52, 85, 88, 114, 116, 119, 133, 148
War of Independence, 67, 116
water, 21, 62
weather forecasting, 143–4
Whitaker, T.K., 126
Whyte, John, 133–4
Wilson, Harold, 40
wind farms, 98
women's movement, 85
working classes, 4, 28, 105–6